As a Christian artist, I am extremely committed to encouraging young people to trust Jesus with every area of their lives. I have been blessed to be able to travel all over the world to communicate this message personally. And of all the areas of Christian life where young people need encouragement, sexual purity is at the top of the list.

So many young people think they will never be hurt in this area, but they are.

Many end up pregnant, get their hearts broken, or catch sexually transmitted diseases.

Satan is very good at tricking people into sexual sin, but God is smarter and has all the answers that young people need to their sex and dating questions. *I Don't Want Your Sex for Now* offers many of those answers. This book will encourage teens to *be* pure, but it will pro   g them how to *stay* pure.

I am glad not only that M   has used a lyric from our song '   title. It makes me feel as though my message to teens is still being preached.

If you are a teen, you must read this book, and then read it again. There is much to learn about this topic, and these principles will be helpful to you for the rest of your life. I am confident God will honor your commitment to remain pure.

If you are a parent, *I Don't Want Your Sex for Now* is a must for your child. I have been a good friend of Miles McPherson for over ten years and believe in his ministry to young people. This book is Miles all the way, straight to the point and full of "the Bible says. . ."

Michael Tait
dc Talk

BOOKS BY MILES McPHERSON

21 Jump-Start Devotional

Bad to the Bone

I Don't Want Your Sex for Now

Parenting the Wild Child

The Power of Believing in Your Child

"You MUST READ this book,
and read it AGAIN."
—Michael Tait of dc Talk

I DON'T WANT
YOUR SEX FOR NOW

Miles
McPherson

BETHANYHOUSE
MINNEAPOLIS, MINNESOTA

Published by Bethany House Publishers
A Ministry of Bethany Fellowship International
11400 Hampshire Avenue South
Bloomington, Minnesota 55438
www.bethanyhouse.com

Printed in the United States of America by
Bethany Press International, Bloomington, Minnesota 55438

Library of Congress Cataloging-in-Publication Data

McPherson, Miles.
    I don't want your sex for now / by Miles McPherson.
        p.   cm.
    ISBN 0-7642-2369-0 (pbk.)
    1. Youth—Sexual behavior—Juvenile literature.   2. Sexual abstinence—Juvenile literature.   3. Sexual abstinence—Religious aspects—Juvenile literature.   I. Title.
    HQ27 .M394   2001
    306.7'0835—dc21   2001002521

MILES McPHERSON is president and founder of Miles Ahead Ministries and speaks to hundreds of thousands of teens and adults each year. A former defensive back with the San Diego Chargers, Miles is a nationally known evangelist and the founder of The Rock Church, which meets at San Diego University. Miles and his wife make their home in San Diego with their three children.

In his ministry Miles has talked to young people from all walks of life—one-on-one and in youth rallies of thousands. He knows what makes them tick, especially rebellious teenagers. That's because he was one. As a junior in high school, Miles started smoking marijuana, which led to cocaine use as a rookie in the NFL. In 1984, however, he committed his life to the Lord. From that point on, he was delivered from his drug habit, stopped using foul language, and was reunited with his girlfriend, Debbie, who is now his wife. After earning a Master of Divinity from Azusa Pacific University, Miles began his ministry and is now a featured speaker at some of the nation's largest youth and adult events. His Miles Ahead Crusades, which target unsaved teenagers, have been used to bring over twenty-seven thousand young people to Christ since 1996.

Miles can be seen live on the Internet Sunday evenings at *www.milesahead.com.*

CONTENTS

I don't want your sex for now . . .

PUBLISHER'S NOTE

The topic of sex never fails to be controversial. Even among Christians, there is disagreement on what is or is not acceptable sexual practice within the context of a marriage relationship. The views in this book are those of the author.

We strongly encourage readers to talk with their parents about sex and to seek their permission before reading this book, as some of the information is explicit and potentially offensive.

INTRODUCTION

In the last fifteen years I have done a lot of Bible teaching, but the topic that I have seen draw the biggest crowds in a church setting has been sexual purity. Thousands come out to learn about sex and dating. It is obvious from this response that Christians and nonbelievers alike want and need to hear as much as possible about what the Bible has to say on this topic.

Because of the overwhelming response the first time I taught this series, I decided to add a component the second time around in order to provide as much help for the people who were coming. Since most of the audience was of high school and college age, I knew that providing counseling would really be helpful. We decided to print names of Christian counselors in our bulletin who would be available to talk to young people about many different kinds of physical and mental issues if there was interest.

Well, the response was overwhelming. The phone of the counseling office rang off the hook. Just hearing me talk encouraged kids to get help for their problems.

I Don't Want Your Sex for Now will bring into light the truth about sex, dating, and many of the issues surrounding the consequences of being sexually active.

Satan has the most leverage against you when he is operating in darkness. As long as he can keep you alone, away from wise Biblical counsel, he can get you to believe his lies all day long.

But God wants to bring things into the light. He wants to give you the best chance to be happy by exposing the deeds of the evil one.

I Don't Want Your Sex for Now will help you establish and maintain sexual purity in your life. Sexual purity means honoring God in all areas of your sexual life. These include the mental, emotional, physical, social, and especially spiritual areas.

The right information will help you make informed and educated decisions about dating, how far you can go sexually, the types of things you should be thinking about, and what you should or should not be wearing or looking at.

I will not only give you good reasons to wait to have sex, but I will also give you ways to protect yourself from giving in to temptation. If you're already sexually active, I will show you how to restore and maintain your virginity. *I Don't Want Your Sex for Now* will provide guidelines that will help you end up in a great relationship—one that is pleasing to God.

The TV shows of today paint a very unrealistic picture of relationships. People fall in love, break up, recover from pain, and get someone new, all in a thirty-minute show. Things in real life just don't happen that way.

I Don't Want Your Sex for Now is designed to help you look at the topics of love, sexuality, and immorality square in the face. Most importantly, this book will help you learn how to love and be loved the way God intended.

Read this book prayerfully, for God has given us a wonderful gift in sex, and it must be enjoyed His way and in His time.

I DON'T WANT YOUR SEX FOR NOW

CHAPTER 1

BECAUSE I JUST FOUND OUT WHAT IT REALLY IS

While driving to Los Angeles from San Diego, I noticed a dog trying to cross the freeway. When I first saw the dog, it was on the opposite side of the freeway, about six hundred feet in front of me. As it began running toward the median, I immediately thought to myself, *Snoop Doggy Dog is not going to make it across the freeway without getting hit.* The speed limit was sixty-five miles per hour; therefore, the cars were actually moving about eighty miles per hour.

As I watched in amazement, the dog made it to the middle of the freeway and was now going to try to cross on my side. I was in the speed lane, and the dog was going to have to go in front of me first. Since it was still about three hundred feet (or a football field length) away, the dog was in no danger of getting hit by me, yet. But there were many other cars it had to try to avoid.

The dog continued to run, making it safely across my lane and the next lane; but in the third lane there was trouble waiting. A young girl was driving a little Fierro and did not see the dog coming. As the dog approached her car, I knew that the girl was going to hit it. By the time she saw the dog and tried to stop her car, it was too late. I saw the smoke coming from her tires at the same time I saw the dog go under the car. In the end, she killed the dog.

You may be asking yourself, *What does this story have to do with sexual purity?* Everything! The only reason this girl hit the dog is because she never saw the dog coming. She just saw the road immediately in front of her. She did not see the big picture. I was able to avoid the dog because I saw him when he was just beginning to run across the freeway. I saw the big picture. When it comes to sex and dating, you must be able to see the big picture—God's picture. When feelings toward the opposite sex arise, real confusion sets in. You like someone, you want to be close to him or her, you want to hold that person, but you must keep the big picture in mind. You must be realistic about God's point of view. After all, He created sex.

We are going to look at many aspects of sex and relationships. I will talk about guy-girl relationships and reasons and ways to stay pure. But the first thing we must agree on is the definition of sex.

WHAT IS SEX?
SHAMELESS ONENESS

While filming a video on sexuality, I asked a group of teen-agers what they thought sex was. I thought I was going to get hands going up all over the place, but everyone sat there, hesitating, wondering if this was a trick question. Well, it wasn't. They were all waiting for someone else to answer the question because no one wanted to get it wrong. After all, they all claimed to be "experts" on the subject, but no one wanted to seem like the fool in the class.

Some eventually said that sex was when a guy and girl "did it." Some said it was "what happens in order to make a baby." I had asked this same question in a junior high school once, and someone said sex was "when two people are under the covers and the bed moves up and down." Others described it as kissing, hugging, holding, and of course, intercourse.

To many people, that is all sex is. It is very true that all of these things are sexual activity, but we are going to keep our eyes focused on the big picture. We are going to have to get God's perspective on what sex is, because there is so much more to it than just kissing and hugging and having intercourse. If you don't keep the big picture in mind, you will be like the dog on the freeway—dead.

The first thing we need to acknowledge about sex is that it is from God. It is good, and it is natural.

The Bible says in Genesis 1:31, "Then God saw everything that He had made, and indeed it was very good."

Many of you may have experienced sex already and wonder

why it could be so wrong if it feels so good. Remember, just because sex may feel good for a season, outside of marriage it is still wrong. The question is, are you being tricked into a few minutes of pleasure that will, in the end, bring lasting pain? Satan is not going to tell you he is ruining your life, but quite the opposite. He is going to do his best to convince you that he is helping you enjoy life. But he's lying to you. That is why it is vitally important to base your decisions on the facts of God's Word, not on how something feels.

The principles outlined in this book will be based on the truth: the Bible. You must decide if you are going to trust God, who the Bible says cannot tell a lie.

Hebrews 6:18 says, ". . . it is impossible for God to lie. . . ."

Or you can believe Satan, whom the Bible calls "the father of lies" (John 8:44 NIV).

Let's keep the first thing first: We must agree that sexual attraction and a person's need for companionship are natural.

One day I was in the grocery store with my son, who was about five years old at the time. When your little kids are quiet for more than thirty seconds, something is wrong. They are either getting into trouble, or they're asleep.

Anyway, I'm in line and he's quiet! I think to myself, *What's he doing?* I look down, and his forehead is turned to a magazine with a pretty woman on the cover. So here's Miles, my son, standing there saying, "Hey, Dad, look at that!" And he pokes the girl on the cover. POW!

At first I was in shock. I thought to myself, *Does he know what he is looking at?* I responded to Miles by saying, "Now, son, you're not supposed to be doing that." But there was another part of me that realized this was a natural reaction for him. There is nothing wrong and everything natural about a guy being attracted to a girl.

"And the Lord God said, 'It is not good that man should be alone; I will make him a helper comparable to him'" (Genesis 2:18).

Let me start at the end of the story. I want you to picture a wedding.

A woman comes down the aisle in a white dress that represents her purity. She's walking with her father because it is her father's job to keep her pure. The father brings the bride down and gives the groom the responsibility of keeping the wife pure—not celibate, but pure. There are three candles on the altar. Two are lit, but the one in the middle is not. The groom takes a candle, the bride takes a candle, and they use their "two fires" to light the one candle, and two fires become "one fire."

Genesis 2:24 says, "Therefore a man shall leave his father and mother and be joined to his wife, and they shall become one flesh."

God unites two people as "one" at the altar. You become one. Think about it. You are married, you walk down the aisle holding hands, and you mingle with the crowd the whole time you are one. You physically disconnect from holding hands, but you are still one. You are no longer dating—you are one.

Consummation of marriage is the ultimate experience of this oneness of a husband and wife. The oneness that comes from spiritual, emotional, physical, and mental union is experienced in God's gift of sex in marriage.

We must realize that sex is not limited to the sexual organs, even though they are often the focus of sexual conversation, pornography, and music videos. Sex, the way God intended it to be expressed, involves the entire person.

God's uniting of two people into "one flesh" means that God makes two people one in marriage, and then He gives them the gift of sex as a means by which they can experience that oneness! In order for the needs of a man and woman to be met completely and correctly, God made it so these two people could be joined into "one person" in marriage. He unites their bodies, their emotions, and their hormones so that they can actually become one person through sexual intimacy. It will be such a glorious experience!

But this sexual encounter in marriage is something special for another reason: It is a covenant, a blood covenant. Let me explain.

In an ideal situation, when a couple gets married, the man and the woman are both virgins. They have never been sexually united as one with anyone else in their lives. When they are married, their spiritual union is sealed with intercourse. In the Old Testament, this union was taken so seriously that it was customary for a young woman to prove her virginity by bleeding on a sheet. It was a blood covenant (or agreement) between herself and her husband. The fact that blood was involved meant that the agreement was very serious and final, not to be broken. Be sure to check out Deuteronomy 22:13–18 for more advice.

In today's world, this Old Testament custom does not exist anymore. A woman's hymen (the membrane that bleeds when ruptured) is often broken before she is married, even if she is a virgin. It can happen due to the many different activities young girls are involved in. In other words, if a girl doesn't bleed on her wedding night, she is not considered in sin as she may have been in Old Testament times. But the point is that God made sexual union a blood covenant—a very serious agreement between two people. He intended for us to take sexual intimacy very seriously.

Some of you ladies and guys have already had sex and have ruined the chance to experience first-time oneness on your wedding night. That's sad, and it breaks God's heart. That is why sex before marriage is wrong before God. That is why when we take sex lightly and jump into bed with just anyone, God wants to shout, "You don't know what you are doing. I didn't create it for that!" But there is hope for those who have given away their virginity to the wrong person. God can restore your spiritual virginity and give you another chance at having a fulfilling relationship with someone you really love.

We have learned so far that sex is oneness. We have learned that it is a blood covenant. But there is still one more important component that cannot be overlooked: Sex, God's way, has no shame.

Genesis 2:25 says, "And they were both naked, the man and his wife, and were not ashamed."

This idea of being naked and not having shame is a very important factor of having sex the way God intended. When two people are united as one, there cannot be room for shame. They must have accepted God's plan for themselves and each other for "shameless oneness" to occur. This shameless oneness is the biblical foundation for sexual intimacy.

Intimacy comes from the Latin word *intimus*, which means innermost layer. This word has a medical application, in that it refers to the innermost layer, or tissue, of the organs inside of our bodies. But in an emotional and spiritual sense, the word intimus applies to the innermost YOU. Who are you really as a person? What are your fears, dreams, and thoughts? What are the things that make you happy and sad? What do you struggle with, and what makes you tick? Being intimate means being able to share these qualities, both positive and negative, with someone else. But you must first be in touch with these things yourself. You must be comfortable with them yourself. You must be able to see yourself for who you are and accept that person without denial or resentment. You must be able to surrender yourself to God without hypocrisy.

"Behold, You desire truth in the inward parts, And in the hidden part You will make me to know wisdom" (Psalm 51:6).

The words "truth in the inward parts" imply *integrity*, something being the same on the inside as it is on the outside. When the inside and outside don't match, you are simply acting. What is another word for someone who is acting? Hypocrite! *The New Unger's Bible Dictionary* defines a hypocrite as "a double person, natural and artificial." Let's think about this for a minute. If you are not the same on the outside as you are on the inside, your relationships with others have little, if any, integrity.

Another way of defining integrity is to say that someone is the same in public as they are in private. If your relationship has little or no integrity, but is built on a foundation of false, fake, and weak intimacy, it will not last. Not only will the relationship not last, it will be a very shallow and painful experience.

The first step toward becoming intimate with someone is to first become intimate with God and allow Him to give you the eternal security only He can offer.

"Search me, O God, and know my heart; Try me, and know my anxieties; And see if there is any wicked way in me, And lead me in the way everlasting" (Psalm 139:23–24).

Many people think intimacy comes from physical closeness, *but this is not true.* Intimacy implies sharing one's innermost self, but this does not necessarily mean the *physical* innermost self. Intimacy can happen when two people are not physically close.

Another myth is that intimacy can happen quickly. The longer two people are together and the more they become comfortable with each other, the more closely their hearts can be knit together and the more intensely they can begin sharing their deepest feelings and fears.

It is over time that this intimacy—sharing one's innermost self—begins to bond two people into one person. Anything done quickly and on a physical level definitely involves deep feelings, but not the shameless oneness that God intends.

Once God can get you to be honest with Him, you can receive from Him what He has to give you—a changed life. Once this change begins to take place and you get in touch with His plan for your life, then you can begin to honestly share the real you. When you can be honest and share the real you with no shame or embarrassment before God and your spouse, you have accomplished shameless oneness in marriage.

A couple who attempts to become one through sex without having been united as one in marriage cannot be considered shameless before God. In true intimacy, there is no sense of shame, guilt, or embarrassment of sharing the true self. Without this, false intimacy occurs.

Hebrews 13:4 says, "Marriage is honorable among all, and the bed undefiled. . . ."

Are you afraid that the real you will be rejected if you are truly intimate? If you are in a relationship with someone, but feel you cannot share the real you because you feel like it is not safe, you will not be able to experience shameless oneness with that person. You may be experiencing physical pleasure, but the shameless oneness God intended for two people who have been made one in marriage is based on true intimacy.

Before you begin the next chapter, reflect on what you've read. It is very important for you to realize that God desires you to be shamelessly one with someone. God's design for sex is that you be able to fully share your heart, mind, body, soul, and spirit with someone. Take a look at the questions listed below and read back through the chapter until you understand the concepts. Shameless oneness is going to be discussed throughout this book. Hopefully, it will be the definition you use through your whole life.

DISCUSSION QUESTIONS

1. The root word for intimacy means innermost layer! What is this word?

   _____

2. How can two people have sex without being intimate?

   _____

   _____

3. Sex, the way God intended it to be, is when two people who are _____ become _____ and there is no

   _____.

4. What would cause shame to be part of sex?

   _____

   _____

5. Is shame determined by how someone feels while having sex? Explain.

   _____

6. Is it God, society, or you who decides whether there is shame in sex? Explain your answer using Bible verses.

   _____

   _____

   _____

   _____

7. What is the basis for what is considered shameful?

   _____

8. What does it mean to be "naked" as defined on page 17?

   _____

9. Why would trying to be intimate sexually be a dangerous thing for two people who are not married?

   _____

   _____

I DON'T WANT
YOUR SEX FOR NOW

CHAPTER 2

NOT UNTIL YOU
LEARN TO LOVE
ME RIGHT

While being interviewed on a radio program in Arkansas, I was asked a very interesting question: "Miles, what would you do if your daughter came home and said she wanted to have sex with her boyfriend?"

The question took me by surprise, and I sat speechless for a while. The interviewer continued to press for an answer. "Miles, there are thousands and thousands of parents listening right now that want to know what you would do."

I answered, "If my daughter came home and asked me that, I would ask her to explain what she thinks sex is and why she thinks sex would satisfy or fulfill her longings. I would also have her process who this guy really was to her."

Then I was asked what I would say to her if she told me she was in love. So the million dollar question is: What does it mean to be in love? How many young girls have been told "I love you" and did not know what that really meant?

Many times young people get crushes, think it's love, and then assume that those feelings justify having sex. They believe having sex will improve, validate, or express those feelings best. Or they might think that having sex is what naturally comes after those feelings are experienced.

As we investigate this thing called love, let's first start with the concept of having a crush on someone, because this is where the confusion often starts.

One time I was at another radio station for an interview, and the woman who greeted me at the front desk had a picture of one of the Backstreet Boys next to her. So I asked, "Who's that guy?"

She said, "Oh, that's my man."

Going along with her, I asked, "Are you dating him?"

She said, "No, but he's THE BOMB!"

Is this what having a crush is all about? A girl sees a guy, she doesn't know him, and there's one thing about him she likes. It could be his ears, his lips, the clothes he wears, his voice, his eyes, his hair, his car, or the power she thinks he has. Once she focuses on that, her mind starts to fantasize that everything else about him is just as perfect. She's got a crush! And he becomes her fantasy.

Even if her friends think he's this dorky guy with high-water pants who doesn't own a comb, she keeps saying, "He is soooo cute!" She's so caught up on wanting to be in love that she's created someone that doesn't exist. After all, no one is perfect. Then the devil tells her that if she can go on a date with that person, she will all of a sudden be better off because of it. It's not true! She may have fun for a little while, but in the end she's going to be let down!

Am I trying to tell you that having a crush is wrong? No! Am I saying that you should avoid having a crush on someone? No! What I am saying is that having a crush and strong feelings for someone is very natural, but it does not mean that you are in love. And strong feelings can't justify your actions.

Being interested in someone because of their outward appearance does not equal love. At some point you might hear a crush tell you, "I love you." But how will you know for sure if the words are genuine?

Let's take a look at what it really means to be in love.

The Bible says the number one commandment in life is to love God with all your heart, mind, and soul. There are two words for love in Greek—well, there are actually three: *eros* love, *phileo* love, and *agape* love. Eros and phileo love are associated with affection and emotions. You love somebody, you want to be with her, you are attracted to her. That's eros and phileo love. Ooey, gooey feelings, okay? Agape love is a whole different story.

Agape love is not based on emotion or a love that expects something in return. Agape love is primarily a love of the will rather than the emotions. The Bible never speaks of God loving people with emotional love or a love that expects something in return. He loves us with agape love, unconditional and unselfish in nature.

Nowhere in the Bible does God command us to phileo love

anybody. The Bible says that we are to agape love our brother. But how does that happen? First, we need to know that we are commanded to love.

Matthew 22:37–40: "Jesus said to him, 'You shall love the Lord your God with all your heart, with all your soul, and with all your mind.' This is the first and great commandment. And the second is like it: 'You shall love your neighbor as yourself.' On these two commandments hang all the Law and the Prophets."

It is biblical to love yourself, but it is vitally important for you to understand what that means. Loving ourselves means we are wanting, desiring, pursuing, and getting what is best for ourselves. And since only God knows what is best for us, only God can deliver it. Therefore, loving ourselves means placing God's plan for our lives first. Since the Bible says the greatest thing we can do is love God, it must be the best way to secure God's best for us. Therefore, the best way to love yourself is to love God.

First John 5:3 says, "For this is the love of God, that we keep His commandments."

It doesn't say that to love God is to just go to church or to love God is to read your Bible. It doesn't say that to love God is to pray every day. No, it says that to love God is to obey Him. That means you are supposed to do what He commands—all the time. By obeying God, you are going to place yourself physically, emotionally, mentally, and spiritually in a place where God can bless you the most.

Now, if you are committed to loving God by obeying Him, every decision you make should first be run by the Lord. For example, if you're really interested in someone, you might say,

"Lord, I'm feeling faint. Is she the one for me?" And God says, "No, you just ate some bad salad last night. Don't go out with her." Then you say, "But, Lord, I'm sweating. I must be feeling something for her." And God replies, "No, you just have a fever." On the other hand, when the right person comes along, God will be the first one to let you know if he or she is the right one. Remember, He loves you and wants only what is best for you.

So far we've learned that to love God means to obey God, and to love ourselves means to obey God, as well.

The second part of Jesus' commandment, "love your neighbor as yourself," is simple to understand. Loving others as ourselves means we want what's best for them. And what's best for each of us is obedience to God. If I want myself to be blessed, I simply make a commitment to obey God. If I want for you the best life God can give you, all I have to do is commit myself to helping you obey God. Remember, it is God, not me or anyone else, who can provide a blessed and fulfilling life. End of story. Being committed to helping someone obey God is the foundation of your love for them.

If I meet you on the street and I say "Man, I love you," you might be thinking in your heart, *You don't love me, you don't even know me.* Well, you are right, in a dating sense or romantic sense. But this is agape love, and it means I want to help you obey God.

Just imagine you have a special friend who wants to get close to you. Each of you has that gleam in your eyes and butterflies in your stomach. This person's arm is around you as you walk down the street, and you think, *Oh, this is so nice.* But all of a sudden he or she asks you to do something that you know would be disobedient to God. Your feelings tell you that it would feel good to keep right on going. They tell you that getting physical will validate your emotions and make the relationship more complete. So what do you do?

It doesn't matter what your feelings say. What does God say?

The Bible says in Romans 1:17, "The just shall live by faith."

In other words, you live and act according to what God's Word says—not what your feelings say. Remember, sin is doing what *you* want and not what *God* wants. And keep in mind that the penalty of sin is death. Pregnancy can bring death to your teenage freedoms, and sexually transmitted diseases can bring death to your health, your ability to have babies, even your life.

If someone really loved you, would that person want you to risk all this just to have sex? That isn't love. That's lust. Lust is a strong desire for something that one does not have. Some people will say or do almost anything to satisfy that desire, even if it means causing someone else to sin.

Lust desires to please self at the expense of others because lust wants to get. On the other hand, love desires to please others at the expense of self. Love wants to give.

When someone tries to get you to do something that would be disobedient to God, he or she lusts you, not loves you. There may be love in that person's heart for you, but the attempt to get you to sin against God is not an act of love but an act of lust.

Luke 17:1–2 says, "Then He said to the disciples, 'It is impossible that no offenses should come, but woe to him through whom they do come! It would be better for him if a millstone were hung around his neck, and he were thrown into the sea, than that he should offend one of these little ones.'"

Satan would love for you to think that you can't be delivered from the stronghold of lust. He also wants you to believe that because your desires are natural, you are off the hook for controlling them. But Satan is wrong.

The Bible says in 1 Corinthians 10:13, "No temptation has overtaken you except such as is common to man; but God is faithful, who will not allow you to be tempted beyond what you are able, but with the temptation will also make the way of escape, that you may be able to bear it."

We are responsible for resisting temptation. But here's the good news: God will never require us to do something that we are not capable of. He will help us find a way out.

So let's get back to my original question. What does it mean to be in love? Ask yourself this: Does this person love me in order to get something or in order to help me obey God? Is he or she praying with me? Reading the Bible with me? Encouraging me in my ministry? Encouraging me in my walk with Christ? Encouraging me to be who God made me to be?

If this person is doing all those things, then he or she has a clear understanding of what love is. Chances are, everything this friend does will be based on that obedience to God.

The one aspect of love that many people forget is that it's a choice. You can and must make a conscious decision to love someone. Whether you help someone obey God or not has nothing to do with your feelings, but is a decision you make.

Even though you may have strong feelings, they should not be what controls you. Feelings are something that must be controlled *by* you. Because your feelings can change day by day and minute by minute, you must base your decisions on something more consistent and stable: the Word of God. Make a decision today that your actions will not be based on your feelings, but they will always be based on the truth of God's Word.

DISCUSSION QUESTIONS

1. Love desires to please _____ at the expense of self, and lust is a desire to please _____ at the expense of others.
2. To love someone is to help them _____ God.
3. List three spiritual qualities that someone would need to possess in order to love you God's way.

   _____

   _____

   _____

4. What are three actions you think you need to avoid in order to remain obedient to God?

   _____

   _____

   _____

5. What three things do you see other teens doing that you now know are not love-based but lust-based?

   _____

   _____

   _____

6. What types of things do you think co-ed friends can do together and still maintain a love for God and each other and not fall into sin?

   _____

   _____

   _____

I DON'T WANT
YOUR SEX FOR NOW

CHAPTER 3

EVEN THOUGH

YOU REALLY,

REALLY WANT

MINE

The most fun times I have while on public school campuses come when I just talk with a group of teenagers. It is during these times that I can really get down and dirty into their business and find out what they are thinking. In turn, they end up asking really personal questions that have been bugging them for some time. One day, while sitting with a group of kids in the gymnasium, the subject of sexuality came up. We talked about many topics, the main one being the issue of how far a person can go without sinning.

A sixteen-year-old girl, whom I happened to know, asked, "Is it a sin to tongue-kiss my boyfriend?" Because I knew the girl, I knew that no matter what I said, she was going to do what she wanted. But I was still responsible for giving her the most biblically accurate answer I could. Before I answered her question, though, I had my own question. I looked her in the eye and asked, "When you finish kissing your boyfriend, are your clothes still on?" She rolled her eyes, flung her hair, and walked away.

When you try to decide how far you can go, the first question you must ask yourself is this: "Am I trying to get as close to the fire as possible without being burned, or am I trying to get as close to God as possible?" As a Christian, your number one goal in life should be to please God with your thoughts and actions.

But let's get back to the girl's question. Even though she walked away, many of the other teenagers wanted to know more. I said, "You can do anything you want as long as it does not cause you to lust."

As soon as I said this, everyone's face changed several times as they thought about what I'd said. At first they were excited. This is exactly what they wanted to hear. But then they began to think the words through. They began to ask even more questions. "What does lust mean?" "How far is that?" "What can I do without lusting?"

All of these questions and everyone's looking for loopholes in my answer caused a lot of confusion. These young people wanted a simple, clear answer like "Don't kiss, don't have intercourse, and don't feel on each other." But the answer goes a lot deeper than that. In order to avoid lust, a person needs to avoid anything that would cause an impure thought or feeling. Remember, holiness is the standard—the only standard.

Matthew 5:27–30 says, "You have heard that it was said to those of old, 'You shall not commit adultery.' But I say to you that whoever looks at a woman to lust for her has already committed adultery with her in his heart. If your right eye causes you to sin, pluck it out and cast it from you; for it is more profitable for you that one of your members perish, than for your whole body to be cast into hell. And if your right hand causes you to sin, cut it off and cast it from you; for it is more profitable for you that one of your members perish, than for your whole body to be cast into hell."

Again, the key word in this verse is lust. I am dedicating an entire chapter to this topic because lust plays a big role in all sexually immoral behavior. I cannot think of one act of sexual sin where lust is not involved, if not totally in control and calling the shots.

About three months after this conversation at the high school, I was talking with a few young people on the same campus again when the girl who asked the question about how far she could go walked by. You guessed it—she was pregnant. I called her over and confirmed that she was indeed preparing to have a baby. I then asked her if she had been kissing her boyfriend. One kiss led to one hug, which led, well, you got it.

Job 31:1 says, "I made a covenant with my eyes not to look lustfully at a girl" (NIV).

If you can make this deal with God and keep it, being sexually pure will be much easier.

Another guideline to live by is this: You should not do anything that causes someone else to sin.

First Corinthians 8:9 says, "But beware lest somehow this liberty of yours become a stumbling block to those who are weak."

There is no way we can know what is in the mind of everyone we come in contact with. But when it comes to the people we hang out with on a regular basis, we usually know when we are crossing the line in the things we say and do.

As a matter of fact, if you are doing things with the specific intent of arousing someone or causing someone to be interested in sexual things, you are being pornographic. The definition of pornography in *Webster's College Dictionary* includes things "intended to arouse sexual excitement."

When you got dressed today, ladies, were you trying to look sexy? Showing a little bit of this, a little bit of that, trying to get some guys or girls to look at you? You may be thinking, "What's wrong with that? This is my body." No, your body is the temple of the Holy Spirit (1 Corinthians 3:16).

God didn't tell you to dress like that, did He? No, MTV told you to do that! The devil wants you to dress like that! What you need to do is make a commitment to God to obey Him in everything, including dressing in a way that is pleasing to Him.

JESUS IS TEMPTED

In Matthew chapter four, Satan tries to tempt Jesus into sin by using the power of lust. Since lust is a strong desire to have something that does not belong to you, it can apply to anything, not just sex. I want to show you how the devil used it against Jesus and how the devil wants to use it against you.

The three areas that Satan tempted Jesus were:

- *The lust of the flesh:* A strong desire for something based on fulfilling a desire of the body.

- *The pride of life:* A strong desire for something based on building up your pride.
- *The lust of the eyes:* A strong desire for something based on getting something you have seen.

First John 2:15–17 says, "Do not love the world or the things in the world. If anyone loves the world, the love of the Father is not in him. For all that is in the world, the lust of the flesh, the lust of the eyes, and the pride of life, is not of the Father but is of the world. And the world is passing away, and the lust of it; but he who does the will of God abides forever."

How is Satan causing you to lust? By building up your pride, by tempting you with what you see, or by convincing you that you can control your own life? As we read about how he tempted Jesus, be thinking about how he is tempting you.

THE LUST OF THE FLESH: A strong desire for something based on fulfilling a desire of the body.

"Then Jesus was led up by the Spirit into the wilderness to be tempted by the devil. And when He had fasted forty days and forty nights, afterward He was hungry. Now when the tempter came to Him, he said, 'If You are the Son of God, command that these stones become bread' " (Matthew 4:1–3).

Jesus fasted in the desert for forty days and forty nights. Obviously, after His fast He was hungry. The Bible goes on to say that the devil came and said, "If you are really God, turn those stones to bread." He was tempting Jesus through the lust of the flesh. In other words, Jesus' flesh—his stomach—was hungry. It had a need, a want: a desire to eat. Satan decided to use this natural desire to entice Jesus to satisfy it on His own by turning the stones to bread.

That was a pretty smart plan. The devil was telling Jesus, "Jesus, you have a natural, God-given need and desire. You're hungry. You have the ability and power to satisfy that God-given need. God gave you the power to satisfy that need by turning the stones to bread because you're God. So why don't you take matters into your own hands and do it?"

Sounds logical, doesn't it? But Jesus wasn't done with His fast yet. Whether or not He could satisfy that need wasn't the point. If God told Him not to eat, He shouldn't eat.

How does this story apply to you? Well, let's look at it this way: You have a natural need and desire to have someone hold you, have someone love you. You have a natural desire to have sex. It's a God-given desire, so what is wrong with satisfying it?

Well, here's the trick. The Bible says we shall walk by faith and not by sight. That means that every day we must get our direction from God. We don't give ourselves direction. That is why it's so important to have our ears tuned to the voice of God in everything we do. To walk by faith, even when tempted, means we obey God in all things and trust Him to meet our needs according to His timetable. That's why I have used so much Scripture in this book, because God's Word is the foundation of all truth, and that includes truth related to sex and dating.

So when you have a desire to kiss, what does the Bible say? "I made a covenant with my eyes not to look lustfully at a girl" or boy (Job 31:1).

When you have a desire to hug, what does the Bible say? "I made a covenant with my eyes not to look lustfully at a girl" or boy (Job 31:1).

When you have a desire to look at a magazine full of women or watch a man walk through the mall, what does the Bible say?

"I made a covenant with my eyes not to look lustfully at a girl" or boy (Job 31:1).

God knows what your needs are. He knows what your wants are. He also has the perfect timetable and perfect person and perfect way to satisfy your needs.

THE PRIDE OF LIFE: A strong desire for something based on building up your pride.

The next temptation Satan tried on Jesus was the pride of life. This is the desire or lust to be DA MAN! The pride of life makes you do things in order to impress others.

"Then the devil took Him up into the holy city, set Him on the pinnacle of the temple, and said to Him, 'If You are the Son of God, throw Yourself down. For it is written: "He shall give His angels charge over You," and, "In their hands they shall bear you up, Lest you dash your foot against a stone"'" (Matthew 4:5–6).

Satan was trying to trick Jesus into impressing people through fame. Sometimes sin is motivated by the desire to look important, cool, or like you've got things together. Satan will tell you that you need these things in order to be lovable. He will tell you that by seeking to impress others you will be important and your need for power will be satisfied.

Are you dating someone or trying to attract someone because of how it is going to make you look in front of other people? If so, then your pride has been calling the shots.

Looking again at Jesus' example in this story, we see Jesus use the Word of God to resist Satan's temptations. "Jesus said to him, 'It is written again, "You shall not tempt the Lord your God"'" (Matthew 4:7).

THE LUST OF THE EYES: A strong desire for something based on getting something you have seen.

"Again, the devil took Him up on an exceedingly high mountain, and showed Him all the kingdoms of the world and their glory. And he said to Him, 'All these things I will give You if You will fall down and worship me' " (Matthew 4:8–9).

Satan will show you the glory of the kingdom, but not the trouble, crime, or problems of the kingdom. Satan is trying to entice you into sin; therefore, he must make it look good. But Jesus responded the way we need to. He said, " 'Away with you, Satan! For it is written, "You shall worship the Lord your God, and Him only you shall serve" ' " (Matthew 4:10).

Looking at sin through rose-colored glasses like Satan wants us to do is exactly what got Samson in trouble. You remember Samson; he had supernatural strength. He also had a thing for women—the lust of the eyes to be specific. Twice the Bible tells us that Samson "saw" a woman and lusted after her for sex. Eventually Samson got a girlfriend named Delilah. Delilah was not walking with God. She was using Samson to get to the secret of his strength. And Samson was so full of lust for her that it cost him his favor with God and eventually his life.

Remember, Satan is not going to show you the consequences of your sin. He'll just show you whatever appeals to your sinful nature.

Tempting and enticing our lusts is the first way Satan attacks. But God is faithful and never will allow us to be tempted beyond what we can overcome. There will never be a circumstance in which you can say, "I could not resist." In the end, you must respond to these temptations in the same way Jesus did. You must use the Word of God as your defense. With the Word of God, you *can* resist the devil.

> *Therefore submit to God. Resist the devil and he will flee from you. Draw near to God and He will draw near to you (James 4:7–8).*

As you deal with your lusts, begin to apply the Word of God to them. Memorize the Word, speak the Word, apply the Word to every lustful thought, and watch how God supernaturally begins to purify your thoughts, feelings, and desires. Keep in mind that no matter what temptations you face, you and you alone will be responsible for how you react.

> *James 1:13–15: "Let no one say when he is tempted, 'I am tempted by God;' for God cannot be tempted by evil, nor does He Himself tempt anyone. But each one is tempted when he is drawn away by his own desires and enticed. Then, when desire has conceived, it gives birth to sin; and sin, when it is full-grown, brings forth death."*

DISCUSSION QUESTIONS

1. If lust is a strong desire to have something that does not belong to you, what kinds of things do you think people will do to get the things that do not belong to them?

   _____

   _____

   _____

   _____

   _____

   _____

2. List three things you have that someone would lust after.

_____

_____

_____

3. Are you doing anything to cause others to lust after these things? For example, have you used words, worn clothes, or flirted in a way to lead others to believe they might get what they want?

_____

_____

4. What do you think will happen once the person gets what he or she is lusting after?

_____

_____

5. If people's actions are determined by their desire to have something that does not belong to them, can you trust their actions?

_____

_____

6. List three things you have seen someone do in order to fulfill their lust for someone.

_____

_____

_____

7. If being pornographic is doing anything that would cause someone to desire sex, list any of the ways you are guilty of this.

_____

_____

_____

I DON'T WANT
YOUR SEX FOR NOW

CHAPTER 4

AND NOW I KNOW

WHY

N o one ever loses their virginity," I told the girls sitting on the wall at lunchtime. They gave me a puzzled look. I continued, "When was the last time you heard someone walking through the halls yelling, 'Hey, dude, have you seen my virginity? I lost it somewhere.' No, you don't lose your virginity. Unless you've been raped, you give it away."

They were quiet, listening for me to say more. I had just finished speaking at their school when I spotted this group of students sitting on the privileged senior wall. I laughed to myself as I watched the very typical interaction. Some guys were throwing their lines at the girls, thinking they were so smooth. The girls were rolling their eyes and giggling. I walked over and struck up a conversation. The girls knew I was a youth pastor at the time, so they started asking questions that led to a discussion about sexual morality. I got their attention with the virginity line, and I went on to tell them that sex is more than kissing and hugging.

Sex is about becoming one with someone. I told them about being united as one, spiritually and emotionally, and how sex is a wonderful physical symbol of that oneness. "But if you have sex outside of God's plan, you will end up losing a part of your soul," I said.

They sat spellbound, letting God's truth sink in. Suddenly, one girl grabbed my arm, dragged me over to another friend, and told her, "You have to listen to this guy. He told us why we shouldn't have sex."

So many young people *want* to be pure, but they don't know why or how to accomplish it. In the next two chapters, I want to focus on what sexual immorality is, why it is wrong, and what God has to say about it.

The first reason you should steer clear of sexual sin is because it carries with it consequences.

SPIRITUAL CONSEQUENCES

First Corinthians 6:18–20 says, "Flee sexual immorality. Every sin that a man does is outside the body, but he who commits sexual immorality sins against his own body. Or do you not know that your body is the temple of the Holy Spirit who is in you, whom you have from God, and you are not your own? For you were bought at a price; therefore glorify God in your body and in your spirit, which are God's."

Sexual sin has consequences that are worse than any other sin. The first and foremost consequence is spiritual. Sexual sin for a Christian is bringing God into a relationship with a harlot.

First Corinthians 6:15–17 says, "Do you not know that your bodies are members of Christ? Shall I then take the members of Christ and make them members of a harlot? Certainly not! Or do you not know that he who is joined to a harlot is one body with her? For 'the two,' He says, 'shall become one flesh.' But he who is joined to the Lord is one spirit with Him."

Think about this. If Jesus is your Savior, He is one with you. If having sex with someone means, among other things, becoming one with that person, you are consequently bringing Jesus into that oneness. If the person you are having sex with is not your spouse, the only person you are biblically supposed to be having sex with, you are bringing Jesus into a sinful union. And this will affect your relationship with God.

Hebrews 13:4 says, "Marriage is honorable among all, and the bed undefiled; but fornicators and adulterers God will judge."

The second consequence is being eternally alienated from God. Many verses in the Bible support this, but I will only list a few.

First Corinthians 6:9–10 says, "Do you not know that the unrighteous will not inherit the kingdom of God? Do not be deceived. Neither fornicators, nor idolaters, nor adulterers, nor homosexuals, nor sodomites, nor thieves, nor covetous, nor drunkards, nor revilers, nor extortioners will inherit the kingdom of God."

Revelation 22:14–15 says, "Blessed are those who do His commandments, that they may have the right to the tree of life, and

*may enter through the gates into the city. But outside are dogs
and sorcerers and sexually immoral and murderers and idolaters,
and whoever loves and practices a lie."*

God's Word is plain and clear. You may be thinking to yourself, "God will understand if I bend one of these rules every now
and then." A lot of people feel that way, but it is wrong.

While talking with a young couple, I felt led to ask, "Are you
two sleeping together?" Both of their faces got red from embarrassment, and then he said, "Yes, we are, but let me explain."

Because I have heard it all and preached against every excuse
in the universe and beyond, I could not wait to hear this one. So
I said, "Speak on, brother."

"I know the Bible says not to have sex before you get married," he said. "But I believe it says this because if you have sex
before you get married, you are committing adultery against your
future wife. Since I am going to marry her, I am not committing
adultery against her. Therefore, having sex right now with her is
not a sin."

I thought to myself, *This is really good. I have never heard this
one before.* Unfortunately, it still doesn't work. All your excuses
and reasoning may seem good to you and may fool lots of people
much of the time, but you are still accountable to God, and He
isn't fooled.

Another time I was speaking to a group of kids in a small
town outside of Detroit. I woke them up when I announced, "I
want to teach you to have good sex—no, GREAT sex." They all
started shouting and screaming, like I knew they would. The
teachers were in a panic, but I knew I'd have them on my side in
a minute.

"Tell me," I began. "Are there rules to sex?"

They all started shouting things like, "No . . . just go with the flow . . . do whatever you want. . . ."

"If there are no rules, can I have sex with my daughter?" I asked. The mood of the room changed abruptly. I knew it hit close to home for some kids. Then they yelled, "No, no . . . that would be wrong."

"I thought you said there were no rules," I responded. "Can I have sex with another man's wife?"

"No," they answered.

"That would break up the family," one girl added.

"Can I have sex with another man?"

"Well, you could," one guy said. "But that would be wrong." The rest nodded in agreement.

Now that they were thinking, I informed them these things weren't wrong for no reason. They're wrong because God said so. Just like most things in life, there are rules, and the same goes for sex. And just like all of life's rules, God designed them. I explained that God made us with sexual desires, but He also gave us guidelines for fulfilling those desires within a healthy, meaningful relationship. The rules and guidelines are given for our benefit, and those rules are found in the Bible. God's requirement is still sexual purity.

While producing a video on sexual purity, I asked a group of high school students if they could have safe sex without being married. Of course they all said yes. As a matter of fact, they thought I was crazy even asking the question. But then I asked them to give me the definition of the term "safe."

Think about that. How can you be free from harm or danger when exposing your heart, soul, and body to someone who is not committed to you for life? How can you be free from harm or danger by doing something that God has clearly said is wrong?

If you sin, you will pay consequences. Period. No questions asked. You must trust that God does not offer idle threats.

PHYSICAL CONSEQUENCES

On another occasion, as I was teaching on sexual purity to a class in an Indianapolis high school, I began receiving a lot of opposition to the validity of sex being dangerous. The students did not deny the fact that sex had its related diseases, which in turn carried with them their own consequences. But the consensus in the classroom was that there were ways to be safe.

In other words, despite the "lethal threat" of those consequences, these kids would still place themselves in situations to enjoy what I have identified in this book as shameless oneness. I want to show you just how wrong they were.

How can you be hurt physically having sex before marriage? A ninth grade boy stood up and shouted, "You can be hurt physically when you have sex with your girlfriend and her father comes after you with a baseball bat!" After the laughter died down, one of the dangers mentioned was sexually transmitted disease (STD). Actually, there are over forty STDs. These diseases can cause blindness in children, sterility in guys and girls, and open sores on the body, the genitals, and mouth. They can even cause death.

Physical dangers are not just restricted to intercourse. I'm often asked if masturbation is wrong. Besides the lust that goes along with masturbation, it is believed by some to carry with it physical danger in that it can hinder ability to perform sexually later on in life. Those who have engaged in masturbation as children and on into adulthood have a higher risk of premature ejaculation. This is not something any person would want to suffer from.

Some young people have decided to engage in anal sex, thinking that they are not actually having intercourse. But in reality, this is a perverted oneness instead of the shameless oneness that Genesis talks about. The rectum was not designed to have anything go into it; this is plainly evident by the physical makeup of it. Anal sex, much more so than vaginal sex, is the cause for the development of many health problems and diseases. This is due to the fact that the rectum is a very polluted area of the body. This kind of sex causes physical harm that you never want to experience.

EMOTIONAL CONSEQUENCES

When I was dating a girl in high school, our relationship started out just fine. We talked on the phone daily, saw each other in school daily, and spent time together after school just about every day. Things seemed to be as good as they could get. I thought about her day and night. I did not think I would ever be with anyone else in my life.

But then problems began popping up. Her old boyfriend began to try to get her back. I began wondering where she was all of the time. Then her family began limiting the time I could spend with her. What started as an uplifting experience was turning into a situation of torture. Jealousy was the main driving force in my life.

I worried about what she was doing and who she was with. I worried about where our relationship was going. I became distracted from my schoolwork, my own family time, and my other friends. The quality of my life was being destroyed because of this emotional hold on my heart.

She was going through the same thing and became jealous of other girls in the school who were my friends.

I have seen teenagers who have become violent over this kind of emotional roller coaster. You have probably even heard of those who have attempted suicide because they could not handle a breakup with someone for whom they had very strong feelings.

Remember, there is nothing wrong with having a relationship with someone of the opposite sex. Hanging out, spending time together, talking on the phone—these are all fine. But when getting too physical happens or oneness is experienced, hearts are knit together and souls become one. Then everything changes. Emotional ties become extremely strong and difficult to break, and that is where the pain comes from.

Because so many people are growing in their knowledge of who they are as a person, their identity can become quickly and strongly wrapped up in the person with whom they become physical. Once you overstep those boundaries, the threat of emotional letdown is tremendous.

Take a moment and write down the ways you can be hurt emotionally by being too physical or having sex too early.

_____

_____

_____

_____

_____

Proverbs 4:23 says, "Keep your heart with all diligence, For out of it spring the issues of life."

In other words, protect the emotional state of your heart. Do everything you can to avoid breaking it. Do what you can to prevent it from being disappointed or let down. Even though these things happen, you can minimize the frequency of them happening by making wise choices. If you look at this verse carefully you'll notice it says, "with all diligence." That implies work. It takes hard work to protect your heart. This is why it is so important to stay committed to God's Word, because it never lies to us.

SOCIAL CONSEQUENCES

Have you ever wondered why some people are attracted to certain people and not to others? One reason is reputation.

Proverbs 22:1 says, "A good name is to be chosen rather than great riches, Loving favor rather than silver and gold."

What are people saying about you because of your sexual behavior? The reputation that your sex life gives you will have far-reaching consequences. Your reputation is going to go before you and follow after you. It is something that is hard to establish and easy to destroy. You can spend a lifetime establishing the trust and respect of your peers, but it only takes one night to ruin it.

When guys and girls are looking to match up, they are going to be drawn to people that represent the type of relationship they desire. Does your reputation represent a wild and sexually crazy evening? Does it represent a relationship that honors God? Guys who want a fast and easy sexual encounter and not much more will be attracted to those girls who have a reputation of being easy to get into bed. There will be times when guys who want a challenge will go after girls who have a good reputation, but that won't happen often once that good reputation is confirmed.

Likewise, the guys and girls who are more committed to staying pure will focus their attention on the people who have the same goals in their life.

What kind of person are you going to be?

Sexual immorality has social consequences among church people also. It will affect your ability to fellowship with other believers if you fail to repent. The Bible tells us that we should not be associated with sexually immoral people, even if they claim to be Christians.

> *First Corinthians 5:9, 11: "I wrote to you in my epistle not to keep company with sexually immoral people. . . . But now I have written to you not to keep company with anyone named a brother, who is a fornicator, or covetous, or an idolater, or a reviler, or a drunkard, or an extortioner—not even to eat with such a person."*

This is God's way of protecting us. He knows that when we hang around with people who are sinning, we will be tempted to sin, too. By steering clear of them, we can save ourselves a lot of heartache.

But what if you are guilty of sexual sin? What can you do to begin repairing the destroyed reputation you have? First, receive forgiveness and cleansing from God. Once your life is right with God, it can become right with others and your reputation can be restored.

> *Proverbs 3:3–4 says, "Let not mercy and truth forsake you; Bind them around your neck, Write them on the tablet of your heart, And so find favor and high esteem in the sight of God and man."*

Another social danger of sexual sin, also a physical danger, is an unplanned pregnancy. Your entire social life is affected forever.

So many teenage girls have babies while in high school and some in junior high school. Instead of focusing just on school, their lives are suddenly consumed by that child for at least eighteen years. It's easy to think babies are cute and wonderful. You can hold and kiss them, but that excitement won't last all day.

In reality, babies require twenty-four-hour care and are up at all hours of the night, seven days a week. You are required to feed the child, change her diaper and clothes, hold her, put her to sleep, wake her up, take her for a walk, play with her, discipline her, and watch her every second she's awake. When the baby gets sick you need to make sure she gets the right medicine at the right times. You need to organize and pay for child care so you can go to school. Any time you want to go out, you have to arrange for and scrape up the money for a baby-sitter.

When and if you go to college, you will have to do this all on your own. When you get out of college, if you go, you will then have to make that much more money to take care of your child's needs as well as your own.

This is a lot of responsibility. And more often than not the father will not be around. In the cases where he is around, he could be an additional drain on your life.

It is also important to remember that the babies that result from sexual immorality are victims of your sin. They didn't ask to come into the world to an unprepared teenage mother, a father that doesn't care, or a less-than-ideal family.

What about the argument that a girl can always get an abortion if she's not ready to become a mom? Check this out:

Day 1: Conception. All forty-six human chromosomes present. A unique human life begins.

Day 7: Embryo begins implanting in the uterus.

Day 22: The heart begins to beat with blood often of a different type than the mother's.

Week 5: The eyes, hands, and feet begin to develop.

Week 6: Brain waves are detectable. Mouth and lips are present.

Week 6.5: All twenty milk buds (teeth) are present.

Week 7: Baby swims freely in the amniotic sac with a natural swimmer's stroke.

Week 8: The beginnings of all body systems are present. Bones begin to form.

Week 9: Baby can suck her thumb, kick, curl her toes, and bend her fingers.

Week 10: Baby is sensitive to touch and has eyelids, fingernails, and fingerprints.

Week 11: Baby can smile. All organ systems are functioning.

Week 15: Toenails form.

Week 17: Baby can dream.

Week 20: Mother feels movements of the baby.

Week 20–22: Baby reaches point of viability, which means survival is possible outside the womb without extraordinary measures.

I am telling you all of this because this complicated process was designed by God, and for a very good reason. When a woman becomes pregnant, God begins to unfold a very beautiful and amazing plan. Aborting a baby and interrupting a pregnancy has negative effects on the woman's health and ability to have babies later on. But most importantly, aborting a baby is wrong. Killing an unborn child is wrong.

Therefore, before you place yourself in a position to cheat a baby out of a chance to live, think twice about the few moments of pleasure and false intimacy that you are going to experience in the process.

I've touched on just a few of the spiritual, physical, emotional, and social consequences of sex. I could go on and on about the dangers, but I think you get the picture. Don't let Satan trick you into thinking a condom can protect you from the consequences of sin. God has something better for you in mind.

DISCUSSION QUESTIONS

1. List a number of ways you can be hurt in the following areas: spiritual, physical, emotional, social.

   _____

   _____

   _____

   _____

2. How can someone have sex and be totally safe, free from harm and danger in all of these areas?

   _____

   _____

3. In what ways have you been hurt or seen someone else hurt from having sex before marriage?

   _____

   _____

   _____

I DON'T WANT
YOUR SEX FOR NOW

CHAPTER 5

AND HERE ARE

SOME MORE

REASONS WHY

F *irst Corinthians 6:18 says, "Flee sexual immorality. . . ."*

That means run! Run from anything that would be considered sexually immoral. The Greek word for flee is *pheugo*. Literally it means to shun, to vanish, or to escape. Flee means to run, hurry away, avoid, and stay clear of. The problem here is being clear on what sexual immorality is. You need to know what you're supposed to flee from.

Sexual immorality covers many things, but before I get into them, let me remind you of the definition of sexual purity. This is when every aspect of your sexual life—whether in thought or action or feeling—is pleasing and honorable to God.

Sexual immorality, on the other hand, includes every aspect of your sexual life that is not honorable to God. The easiest way to abide by the guidelines for sexual purity is to make a commitment to be pure and walk closely with God. But because so many people get caught up in wanting to clarify things and define absolutes, I will lay out a list of sins that you can be sure are considered immoral behavior. Still, there is one thing to always keep in mind: If God says something is wrong and requires that you flee and abstain from it, He will always provide a way to do exactly that. It is your responsibility to believe this assurance and submit to Him by faith.

LUSTING IN YOUR HEART FOR SOMEONE

Matthew 5:27–28 says, "You have heard that it was said to those of old, 'You shall not commit adultery.' But I say to you that whoever looks at a woman to lust for her has already committed adultery with her in his heart."

This is probably one of the most important rules to practice and understand because it will be a guide to all of the unclear issues you face. Lust is a strong desire to have something that is not yours. This includes *anything* that would cause *you* to begin desiring. For some people, steering clear of lust means not holding hands, for others it means avoiding pornographic pictures, for others it means turning off certain television shows or keeping their distance from someone they are attracted to. In the end, the Bible clearly tells us that lusting is wrong and that we need to do whatever we can to avoid it. Other actions creating lust might include kissing, hugging, or looking someone in the eyes for more than five seconds. You might think I'm being ridiculous, but if one of these causes you to lust, you'd better not do it.

Some more obvious things to avoid include feeling someone's genitalia, talking nasty to someone, writing sexually explicit letters or emails, sending sexually explicit pictures or drawings, making sexual gestures, masturbating, fantasizing about someone, looking at any kind of pornography, or engaging in oral, anal, and vaginal sex.

SEX WITH SOMEONE OF THE SAME GENDER, OR HOMOSEXUALITY

While sitting on an airplane, I struck up a conversation with the guy next to me. After a while I asked him if he was married. He responded no. I then asked him if he had a girlfriend. He had talked so much about the house, the car, the money, and the successful business he had I figured there was a woman somewhere in his life. He responded in a way that I was not expecting. He told me he was gay.

Here was a successful young man, who was very friendly, so you may ask, "How could his lifestyle be so wrong? What's the big deal?"

The big deal is this: God says that it is wrong.

Romans 1:24–27 says, "Therefore God also gave them up to uncleanness, in the lusts of their hearts, to dishonor their bodies among themselves, who exchanged the truth of God for the lie, and worshiped and served the creature rather than the Creator, who is blessed forever. Amen. For this reason God gave them up to vile passions. For even their women exchanged the natural use for what is against nature. Likewise also the men, leaving the natural use of the woman, burned in their lust for one another,

men with men committing what is shameful, and receiving in
themselves the penalty of their error which was due."

I have often heard of gay people who claim that they have
been gay as far back as they can remember. Unfortunately, in
many cases, counselors have discovered this is a result of something that happened to these people as children that confused
their sexual orientation. They were molested, raped, or had a dys-
functional relationship with another adult, and their sexual orientation became forever distorted.

No matter someone's reason for being gay, homosexuality is
wrong in the eyes of God. God condemns the lifestyle, but He
still loves the person. Being delivered is possible.

INCEST

" 'No one is to approach any close relative to have sexual relations.
I am the Lord' " (Leviticus 18:6 NIV*).*

Incest is any sexual relationship with any family member.
This problem is so widespread because so many young victims of
incest are afraid to say anything. They don't want to destroy their
families. But in the meantime, they themselves are being destroyed through such abuse. If you are a victim of incest, the scars
you carry will be with you for life unless you do something about
ending the abuse. Only then can you begin healing from its pain.

RAPE

Rape is defined as forcing another person to have sexual intercourse. It doesn't matter how long you've been dating, how
much money he's spent on you, or what he's promised. No one
has the right to force you into sex. It's wrong! In addition, being

forced into any sexual activity against your will is sexual assault. I will cover this topic more extensively in Chapter 7.

PROSTITUTION

This involves paying someone for a sexual favor of any kind. God created sex to be shared between a husband and wife. He never wanted it to be reduced to a favor to be bought or sold.

> *Proverbs 6:25–26 says, "Do not lust in your heart after her beauty or let her captivate you with her eyes, for the prostitute reduces you to a loaf of bread, and the adulteress preys upon your very life." (NIV)*

ANAL SEX

The Bible refers to this as an unnatural lust. In biblical times it was unfortunately used as a pagan religious rite. Today, many young people engage in anal sex because they believe that they can get away with it and still be virgins. Not only are they not virgins, but this kind of sex is an abomination to God.

> *Judges 19:22–23 says, "As they were enjoying themselves, suddenly certain men of the city, perverted men, surrounded the house and beat on the door. They spoke to the master of the house, the old man, saying, 'Bring out the man who came to your house, that we may know him carnally!' But the man, the master of the house, went out to them and said to them, 'No, my brethren! I beg you, do not act so wickedly! Seeing this man has come into my house, do not commit this outrage.'"*

ORAL SEX

Virginity is more than an issue of intercourse; it is an issue of the heart and mind. Oral sex is definitely breaking the spiritual and emotional barrier of what would be considered virginity. So many young people are having oral sex thinking that they are still virgins. Oral sex is wrong for those whom God has not made one.

Satan, who is more intelligent and cunning than you, has very powerful tools when it comes to destroying your life. Satan wants to get you to a house party where there are all kinds of things going on that he wants you to do—drinking, sex, drugs, cursing. He will deceive you into sexual sin any way he can. That is why it is so important to have people in your life who love you and understand his ways a little better than you. Sometimes this understanding comes simply from being older and having seen more.

While at a youth camp on the west coast, I was teaching about sexual purity to a group of teenagers. After the lesson, I opened the time up to a question-and-answer period. One young lady asked, "If my parents trusted me, they would let me go to parties and date boys my age. I am fifteen and know what I am doing."

I have heard this argument so many times, and I used it myself when I was young. But the problem is not just a trust issue. When you are young and living under someone else's authority, someone who is responsible for you, you must realize that they have the last say.

I answered her by saying, "If they trusted you, should they allow you to fly a 747? No, because it is their responsibility to keep you out of harm's way, and there is no way you can fly the plane. No matter how much they trust you and love you, there are certain things they won't allow you to do."

Your parents are aware of Satan's tools and weapons, and it is their job to protect you from them. Likewise, there is a time when sex, love, and everything that goes along with it will be safe and fun, but that time is not until God says so. So until then, steer clear of sexual immorality.

> *"I charge you, O daughters of Jerusalem, By the gazelles or by the does of the field, Do not stir up nor awaken love Until it pleases"* *(Song of Solomon 3:5).*

DISCUSSION QUESTIONS

1. Who established the rules for sex?

   _____

2. What are the consequences of breaking God's rules? See Romans 6:23.

   _____

   _____

3. Is there any way that God's rules could be outdated or not relevant for you today? See Luke 21:33.

   _____

4. List five general rules about sexual sin that the Bible says not to break. Try to find the corresponding verse.

   _____

   _____

   _____

   _____

   _____

5. Explain why sexual sin is worse than all other sins.

   _____

   _____

6. If sex is when two people become one, what spiritual offense against God is made when two people who are not married to each other have sex? See 1 Corinthians 6:15–17.

_____

_____

7. Does breaking God's rules bring pain or pleasure into someone's life? Explain and give examples.

_____

_____

_____

_____

_____

CHAPTER 6

EVEN THOUGH IT

IS ONLY IN MY

MIND

While I was talking with a friend about his testimony, he began to share with me his struggles with sexual addiction. He also shared with me the struggles that his wife had before they got married, how God brought them together, and how He gave them a wonderful marriage and family. I asked how he had dealt with his addiction, and he shared that he had gone to an organization specifically designed for people who are addicted to sex.

At the time I had never heard of such a program and asked what they did to help him. As he explained the program to me,

I was amazed at all the different ways a person could become addicted to sex. There were some people who were into pornographic magazines and videos only. There were others whose addiction was limited to prostitutes. Some of the people were into married women, while others were hooked on child pornography. The classes were specialized to the addiction of the person.

Isn't Satan smart? He will design a million ways to ruin your life.

If I were to ask you what the most powerful sex organ was, what would you say? The heart? The hands? The eyes? No! The answer is the brain! The power of the mind is central to sex—from a person initially thinking of sex all the way to his or her body's response to physical union. The brain has potential beyond what we can imagine or tap into, and its role in sex is often underrated.

Because your brain is the most powerful sex organ you have, it needs to be treated carefully. The brain's huge potential can be both good and bad. In other words, the mind, if used correctly, can be a huge blessing in a person's sex life. But if it is subjected to sexually immoral behavior, the mind can also turn against you. The mind can be used by Satan to bring a great deal of torment into your life. All he has to do is get into your mind, and things go downhill from there. That's what happened to the boy in the following story.

Jason was a fourteen-year-old with low self-esteem who began surfing the Internet. Because of his loneliness, he was searching for love and companionship. He found it in a chat room with a woman named Sheila.

Sheila was a thirty-year-old mother of two who also had loneliness issues. What began as innocent chatting online led to her sending a picture of herself over the Internet. From there, the situation snowballed to sexual fantasies and sexually suggestive conversation.

This led to letters and more pictures. They eventually exchanged phone numbers and spoke for four to five hours per day on the phone. She told him that he was the sexiest guy and that he turned her on. She told him that she could not wait to meet him.

After eight months of flirting on the Internet, they met in a neutral city and spent two nights in a hotel. Sheila was later arrested and faced thirty years in prison. It's important to note that the sex that resulted was something that had started in their *minds*.

Satan will play with your mind and tell you anything you want to hear. His main goal is to destroy your life. I have listed a few statistics that illustrate how much Satan is filling your mind with sexual images. (See page 124 for a list of sources.)

- In its May 2000 ruling of *United States v. Playboy Entertainment Group, Inc.*, the U.S. Supreme Court ruled that cable operators are not required to scramble or fully block porn channels in homes that do not subscribe. Twenty-two to twenty-nine million children live in homes that mistakenly receive such pornography.
- On network TV: One scene containing sexual behavior or discussion occurs every four minutes. On cable TV: Three sexual scenes occur every four minutes, one of which is considered "hard core" (showing sexual intercourse or oral sex).
- Ninety-eight percent of all sexual behavior on TV has no physical consequence. Ninety-six percent of all sexual

behavior in movies or on TV occurs with no judgment of right or wrong. Three out of every four participants in sexual activity in movies or on TV are unmarried.

- Music videos: There are 1.5 sexual scenes per minute.
- Female characters on TV who are under age eighteen engage in sexual interaction in 25.6 percent of their prime time appearances (16.9 percent for males). Female characters from ages eighteen to thirty-nine have sexual interaction in 39.1 percent of their appearances.
- Compared to 1989, in 1999 sexual material was three times as frequent, homosexual references were twenty-four times more common, and references to genitalia were seven times more frequent.
- The movie rating PG allows for brief nudity. PG–13 allows nudity if not in a "sexually oriented" manner. The use of some sexual expletives is also allowed.
- In the year 2000, adult video and DVD sales topped $10 billion, and porn is now "the top business on the Internet."
- Every day up to 30 million people log on to pornographic Web sites.
- Fifteen percent of Web users (9.6 million) logged on to at least one of the ten most popular cybersex sites in one month.

It is foolish to think that the reality behind these statistics is not having an effect on you.

When young children are brought in to counseling sessions because they have been sexually exploited, they are often in great pain and torment. It is not always because someone touched them or physically assaulted them. It is often because someone simply exposed his or her sexual organs to them. When someone's nakedness is uncovered, the image that is placed on the mind of the child might torment them for months, years, or if not dealt with properly, even a lifetime. The mind is so powerful in its ability to keep these images that it is hard to erase the experience.

What is worse is that the brain replays the experience of sexual exploitation over and over again. This replay not only includes the physical images seen with the eyes, but the feelings, fears, anger, and hurt that go along with these images.

Imagine what happens when you, as a teenager, have sex. Think about all of the information that is collected and processed by your brain. Your eyes see the nakedness of someone to whom you are not married. Your nose collects scents related to this sexual sin.

Remember, if your brain is the most *powerful* sex organ, your skin, which covers your entire body, is by far your *largest* sex organ. Therefore, your hands and the rest of your body gather information all to be stored in the mind.

Your ears are another way of gathering information for the brain. They will gather sounds that will become stored in the brain for later recall. Your mouth will collect information in the form of taste and feeling.

After just one sexual encounter, your brain has information from the nose, the skin, the eyes, the ears, and the mouth. Satan can and will use it all to stir up feelings and emotions that will drive you to do almost anything to have this experience again. Satan will also whisper lies into your mind about how fulfilling sex can be.

Even if your sexual encounter was the not the best, Satan will do anything to convince you that the next time will be better. In the cases where you had a bad experience, Satan might use the pain to tempt you to do something sinful to forget or erase the pain, such as get high, have another sexual encounter with someone else, or harm yourself. Satan is really good at what he does. He destroys lives with the lies and deceit of half-truths.

But keep in mind that God is even better at what He does. He's out to save lives. He knows what He is talking about when He tells you to wait to have sex. God knows how to secure the best sex and intimacy in your life by waiting for the right person in the right context: marriage.

This is why Solomon warns us not to awaken these feelings before the time is right.

"O daughters of Jerusalem, By the gazelles or by the does of the field, Do not stir up nor awaken love Until it pleases" (Song of Solomon 2:7).

Even when you experience sex in the biblical way, all your images and memories from past experiences will torment you. They can and will be used to destroy the happiness and joy sex was intended to bring into your life.

Matthew 6:22–23 says, "The lamp of the body is the eye. If therefore your eye is good, your whole body will be full of light. But if your eye is bad, your whole body will be full of darkness. If therefore the light that is in you is darkness, how great is that darkness!"

The emotional torment resulting from past sexual sin can happen even when the images have not been seen with the physical eye. Take the example of Lewis.

Lewis was dating a girl whom he was very interested in. He

decided to investigate her past. He wanted to know more about her previous sexual encounters and partners. Expecting her to have a tame past, he was not prepared for what he heard. She began to explain to him that she had had sex with many men.

Since she had given him such a wild picture of her actions, he decided to ask her about the things that she still thought about doing. She shared with him some of her sexual fantasies, and this was even more disturbing. These fantasies carried with them images that he did not want to have in his mind, especially when they were related to someone he cared about and wanted to spend time with.

By the time I spoke with Lewis, several weeks had gone by, and he could not get these thoughts and images out of his mind.

The things you think about are going to be the things that influence your behavior and your feelings. The images in your mind that pop up will, over time, affect every area of your life. That is why you must take these thoughts and make them obedient to the Lord.

Second Corinthians 10:4–5 says, "For the weapons of our warfare are not carnal but mighty in God for pulling down strongholds, casting down arguments and every high thing that exalts itself against the knowledge of God, bringing every thought into captivity to the obedience of Christ."

Every thought must be considered a source of sin. But as this verse suggests, we have the choice to hand those thoughts over to God. If we bring them into His captivity, we don't have to worry about them anymore. And God will help us think about the good stuff, instead.

Philippians 4:8–9 says, "Finally, brethren, whatever things are true, whatever things are noble, whatever things are just, whatever things are pure, whatever things are lovely, whatever things are of good report, if there is any virtue and if there is anything praiseworthy—meditate on these things. The things which you learned and received and heard and saw in me, these do, and the God of peace will be with you."

The power of lust relies on the brain's capacity to imagine. With these thoughts we create scenarios, actions, and feelings that may never happen—but they cause our hearts to desire things that are sinful. In the end, our entire minds must be renewed, purified, and cleansed so that God's will can be done in our lives.

Let me end with another Bible verse.

Romans 12:1–2 says, "I beseech you therefore, brethren, by the mercies of God, that you present your bodies a living sacrifice, holy, acceptable to God, which is your reasonable service. And do not be conformed to this world, but be transformed by the renewing of your mind, that you may prove what is that good and acceptable and perfect will of God."

Remember, once Satan has gotten into your mind—your most powerful sex organ—he can lead you in almost any direction that he wants. When someone tells you that you can have sex and still be safe, free from harm or danger, ask them what contraception can protect your mind.

DISCUSSION QUESTIONS

1. What types of situations cause you to think about sex? Television shows, music, music videos?

   _____

   _____

   _____

2. Are there particular people who are associated with these thoughts?

   _____

   _____

   _____

3. What sexually immoral images are on your mind that you would love to get rid of?

   _____

   _____

4. In an effort to have your mind renewed, write these three verses down and carry them around with you. Make a commitment to read them when these thoughts come to your mind.

- Romans 12:1–2—"I beseech you therefore, brethren, by the mercies of God, that you present your bodies a living sacrifice, holy, acceptable to God, which is your reasonable service. And do not be conformed to this world, but be transformed by the renewing of your mind, that you may prove what is that good and acceptable and perfect will of God."
- 2 Corinthians 10:4–5—"For the weapons of our warfare are not carnal but mighty in God for pulling down strongholds, casting down arguments and every high thing that exalts itself against the knowledge of God, bringing every thought

into captivity to the obedience of Christ."

- Philippians 4:8–9—"Finally, brethren, whatever things are true, whatever things are noble, whatever things are just, whatever things are pure, whatever things are lovely, whatever things are of good report, if there is any virtue and if there is anything praiseworthy—meditate on these things. The things, which you learned and received and heard and saw in me, these do, and the God of peace will be with you."

I DON'T WANT
YOUR SEX FOR NOW

CHAPTER 7

BECAUSE FIRST
I MUST HEAL
FROM THE LAST
TIME

J ennifer was eight years old when she was first molested. At fifteen she was also raped.

"Growing up you see rape and molestation on television. You hear about it all the time, but you never expect it to happen to you, ever," she said as she shared her testimony. "When I was molested, I was being baby-sat by my uncle. He told my brothers to go to bed because I was the one that was being the good girl. As it was happening I knew something wasn't right, and as soon as my parents came home I reported it to them. But he snuck out

71

the door, and I didn't see him again until I was twenty. The circumstances surrounding another incident involved a different family member, and it happened more than once. I felt as though it were my fault. I always blamed myself. When I was fifteen I ran away, and I didn't know anybody where I was staying. I got drunk and was raped in front of ten other guys. During the assault I experienced a lot of fear. And afterward I felt guilt, like it was all my fault. I had so much hatred toward the people who committed these crimes against me and absolutely no forgiveness."

The story you just read happens every day. According to a study conducted by the National Institute of Mental Health, every forty-five seconds there is a rape in this country. One out of every three girls and one out of every six boys will be sexually abused before the age of eighteen. One out of every two women will be a victim of sexual assault in her lifetime.

Molestation happens whenever someone's sexual privacy is invaded against that person's will. When an adult or older youth sexually uses a child in any way, this is called child molestation. Rape refers to sexual activity that one person pushes on another through physical force or coercion against the victim's will.

Even though this chapter will deal with recovering from an assault, I want to challenge everyone to take to heart the lessons taught. Many, if not all of us, will have our hearts broken. We will go through a painful experience from a relationship. Believe it or not, there are similarities between the experience of Jennifer and those who have simply been hurt through a relationship. Young people, ladies in most cases, are taken advantage of.

In no way do I want to make light of the horror of rape and molestation, but I think there are lessons we can all learn from these terrible crimes. These lessons are based on the similarities of the manipulation that occurs in welcome and unwelcome sexual encounters. My goal is to reveal a few insights into dealing with the pain that results from such manipulation.

I want to use as an outline for this chapter a story from the Bible, in which Tamar is raped by Amnon. There are several valuable lessons we can learn from this story.

Amnon is the son of David. Tamar is also the daughter of David, the half sister of Amnon. The Bible says that Amnon loved Tamar so much that he was distressed to the point of becoming sick. Now, let me tell you something: Love does not make you sick. If you're getting sick over a guy or a girl, it isn't love. That's nothing but lust.

Remember, lust is a strong desire for something that doesn't belong to you. Lust desires to please self at the expense of others because lust wants to get. Love, on the other hand, desires to please somebody else at the expense of self because love wants to give. I told you before and I will tell you again, to love somebody is to be committed to helping them obey God. In many relationships, once sex becomes a goal, dishonest and crafty behavior and bad attitudes begin to dictate behavior.

This is exactly what happened to Amnon. He had a strong desire to have sex with his half sister, and he created a plan to make it happen. Rape and molestation are not spontaneous but premeditated. The person committing the crime—which is what rape and molestation are—thinks it through very carefully. Watch as Amnon follows through on his plan to rape Tamar.

Amnon lures Tamar into his bedroom by claiming to be sick, and then he grabs her and rapes her. The Bible says she asked him to stop but he would not. "However, he would not heed her voice; and being stronger than she, he forced her and laid with her. Then Amnon hated her exceedingly, so that the hatred with which he hated her was greater than the love with which he had loved her. And Amnon said to her, 'Arise, be gone!' " (2 Samuel 13:14–15).

This is where it gets really ugly. Thinking only about himself, Amnon has no idea of the magnitude of the scar he is about to leave on the heart of Tamar.

Tamar says, "No, indeed! This evil of sending me away is worse than the other that you did to me" (2 Samuel 13:16).

Tamar, having just been raped, is now being dumped. She is despised and hated by the guy who just used and abused her. All she's left with is her shame and guilt.

A person can be sexually assaulted without even being touched. Someone can expose himself or herself to you or show you offensive pictures. Some of you reading this book right now have experienced an assault—whether through rape, molestation, or exposure. And others of you are currently in dating relationships where someone is trying to take advantage of you on an emotional or physical level.

In order to better understand why this happens, we need to dispel some of the myths that surround rape. Focus on the Family, in an online article identifying resources for rape victims, included the following misconceptions about rape.

MYTH #1: It's an expression of intense sexual desire.

Rape is a violent crime of aggression of one person against another, end of story! Guys might give you all kinds of lines like "I have needs" or "I want to show you how much I love you." Don't believe that trash! God gave us needs, but He also gave us self-control.

MYTH #2: Rape is always spontaneous.

Up to seventy-four percent of all attackers know their victims. Rape is almost always planned and premeditated. So don't think to yourself, *He was just overcome in the heat of the moment, and I should forget about it.* No, he committed a crime. Don't ever think that someone has spontaneous feelings that cannot be controlled. If you are dating someone who claims such feelings, you are in trouble because he can justify any action by saying, "I couldn't help myself."

MYTH #3: Some women secretly desire or invite rape.

No one would ever desire to be violated in this way. The life-long pain that occurs after rape is nothing anyone would want to bring upon himself of herself. Don't ever let anyone else try to tell you what you want. Let your yes be yes and your no be no.

MYTH #4: Some women deserve to be raped because of their actions.

The belief that some women deserve to be raped because of how they dress or because of where they go is ridiculous. No one ever deserves to be raped. Now, does the way you dress send a certain message? Yes. But it never justifies rape.

When children are molested, they are violated sexually by someone against whom they have no control to stop. One sad thing that can occur is that a child's body can still respond to the advances of the person doing the molesting. In other words, a person's sexual response mechanisms do not automatically shut themselves off just because they are being molested. This sends a very confusing message to the victim.

But what happens after the molestation is the real evil of the crime. Once these sexual response mechanisms have been set in motion through the molestation, they now become prematurely active. This can lead to the misunderstanding of the priority of sex in all relationships. It will also, in a sense, awaken hormones that can lead to a more sexually minded and active person.

Many young girls who are molested will be led to believe, through this crime against them, that the best way to get attention from men is through sex. *It is vitally important to understand that no matter what has happened, you are a victim and it is not your fault.*

Once Satan begins to use this sense of guilt and shame to discourage people, he plays games with their minds. He begins telling them horrible things about their self-worth, their future, and their ability to have a happy relationship. All based on lies, of course. Some of the things Satan will attack are a person's self-confidence, the ability to be normal and happy, opportunities for success, and his or her relationship with God.

A person who has been sexually violated may begin to ask: Where was God when this happened? Can I trust God? Why didn't He help me?

> *Matthew 7:9–11 says, "Or what man is there among you who, if his son asks for bread, will give him a stone? Or if he asks for a fish, will he give him a serpent? If you then, being evil, know how to give good gifts to your children, how much more will your Father who is in heaven give good things to those who ask Him!"*

In this passage Jesus is trying to teach that, as your heavenly Father, God is going to treat you better than any father on earth ever could. Fathers and people on earth are sinful. They're going to let you down. But God will always be there for you!

Proverbs 18:10 says, "The name of the Lord is a strong tower. The righteous run to it and are safe."

If you have been sexually assaulted in any way, the person who hurt you used his or her free will to do evil. But *you* have the ability to use *your* free will to seek God's comfort and healing.

A few years ago I spoke at a Christian camp for a college ministry. I had my own kids with me, and we were running around the field with some college students. One of the young women approached me. After confiding in me that she had been molested, she asked, "Do you think I could ever be a good mom?"

I answered, "Oh, most definitely! God is going to use that negative experience you were victimized with to make you into a great mom."

This young lady had such a negative view of her life and her ability to be a strong parent. All of it was based on what Satan was telling her. But God can turn around what the devil means for evil. He turns it around for good if you let Him.

Sexual assault is not limited to girls. A young man once wrote to me, saying, *I was molested by a guy I have grown up with. He has repented and wants to be friends with me. Though I have forgiven him, I do not want to have a relationship with him. My parents and his parents are saying that if I really forgave him I would continue the friendship, but being friends with him terrifies me. Is what I'm feeling wrong?*

Sometimes people will act like an assault is no big deal and tell you that you need to get over it. Others may accuse you of making the whole thing up. They act like it never happened. Let's look again to the Bible to see what happened to Tamar.

"He [Amnon] called his servant who attended him, and said, 'Here! Put this woman out, away from me, and bolt the door behind her.' Now she had on a robe of many colors, for the king's virgin daughters wore such apparel. And his servant put her out and bolted the door behind her. Then Tamar put ashes on her head, and tore her robe of many colors that was on her, and laid her hand on her head and went away crying bitterly. And Absalom her brother said to her, 'Has Amnon your brother been with you? But now hold your peace, my sister. He is your brother; do not take this thing to heart.' So Tamar remained desolate in her brother Absalom's house" (2 Samuel 13:17–20).

If you have ever been the victim of sexual assault, acting like nothing happened is not going to solve anything. Family members and friends telling you to just forget it isn't the answer, either. First you need time to heal. Then you can work back into the relationship on God's terms as He directs your heart. You are not required to be friends with someone who has violated you. But you are required to forgive them.

"For if you forgive men their trespasses, your heavenly Father will also forgive you. But if you do not forgive men their trespasses, neither will your Father forgive your trespasses" (Matthew 6:14–15).

The first thing you've got to do is receive from God the ability to forgive. Forgiving someone is not saying, "You wronged me and it's okay." Forgiveness is saying, "You wronged me and it hurt, but I am no longer holding you responsible to fix me. I am not going to hold you responsible to heal my pain. I am not going to wait for you to apologize in such a way that I feel better. I am going to release you of that responsibility and move on with my life." That's forgiveness. It's releasing it to the Lord.

Some of you reading this need to release your sinful habits to God. Others of you need to release your pain or anger by giving it to God. Some of you have been manipulating and taking advantage of others. Some of you need to repent of your lust.

Some of you find yourself living a life of desolation, alone, hiding your pain in the secret place in your heart where no one can see it. But let me tell you, God knows and He loves you. Don't allow Satan to keep you desolate and alone, full of shame and guilt. Don't let Satan tell you you're the only one who feels this way.

God wants to deliver you and set you free!

Step one is to tell someone who is safe—someone you can trust to lead you to get the help you need. If you were sexually assaulted by someone inside the family, you might need to tell someone outside the family. Be prepared that your family might have a hard time accepting the truth.

Step two is to get professional help. Molestation and rape are not just physical hurts. They are emotional and spiritual hurts. The access to your heart and soul was violated, and that is why the hurt is so bad and can last so long.

Proverbs 4:23 says, "Keep your heart with all diligence, for out of it spring the issues of life."

Do all you can to maintain the health of your heart. It takes work to not only protect your heart from pain, but to place yourself in a position for the pain to be healed. You cannot ignore this kind of pain and think that it will go away. It takes a concentrated and deliberate effort.

Before you move on to the next chapter, read the discussion

questions carefully and act as soon as possible on any one of them that applies to you. The topics in this chapter are very serious, and the pain of being violated is something that can burden you for your entire life. Don't let this pain ruin you or your future relationships.

DISCUSSION QUESTIONS

1. Have you been sexually violated in any way?

   _____

   _____

2. Are you secretly harboring pain from an assault that you need to be healed of?

   _____

   _____

3. Do you feel as though you have pain from an assault that is not going away, but you would like it to?

   _____

   _____

"Come to Me, all you who labor and are heavy laden, and I will give you rest. Take My yoke upon you and learn from Me, for I am gentle and lowly in heart, and you will find rest for your souls. For My yoke is easy and My burden is light" (Matthew 11:28–30).

I DON'T WANT
YOUR SEX FOR NOW

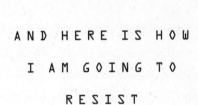

CHAPTER 8

AND HERE IS HOW

I AM GOING TO

RESIST

A fter teaching sexual purity to a group of teenagers, I was
approached by a young girl who had a very serious look
on her face. As she ran through the list of issues that I had cov-
ered, I began to wonder if she was having problems with all of
them. But that was not the case.

She said, "Miles, I believe that what you taught was biblically
correct, but how do you do it?"

Confused, I asked her, "Do what?"

She said, "Stay pure! My friends and I want to stay pure, but
we need some practical guidelines on how to do it."

There are some who would just tell young people not to date, and I think that that is a very safe way to go about things. But there will always be those who are going to develop dating relationships. There must be some room to have some kind of relationship with a person of the opposite sex.

As adults, we need to prepare young people to live responsible lives without assuming that they cannot do it. I have seen young people successfully be friends and spend quality time together without falling, but it takes hard work and the teamwork of many godly people. On the other hand, there are some young people who need to be locked up in a closet until they are married. This is the case with my three children!

There will be people who come into your life with whom you want to have some kind of relationship. Therefore, I have outlined some guidelines for you that, *if followed carefully*, can help protect you from being hurt.

The first step in maintaining your purity is to respect the seriousness of relationships. The second step is to realize that you cannot do this alone. Don't think that you are going to avoid all the traps that Satan has set. Don't think that it cannot happen to you. Remember, Satan is the destroyer. It's his ultimate goal. He wants to destroy as much as possible in your life.

"Therefore let him who thinks he stands take heed lest he fall" (1 Corinthians 10:12).

You are bound to sexual purity your whole life. When you get married, some of these guidelines will not be needed, but some of them will be important for a lifetime. Even if they don't apply to you, they will apply your children. Avoiding sexual immorality does not only apply while in high school; it should last your entire single life.

Remember that it is God, not your parents, who sets the standard for your behavior. Therefore, my prayer is that this chapter, along with the rest of the book, will help you in all of your relationship issues for years to come.

God wants you to know that you should never think yourself above the power of temptation that ruins so many lives of young people. Once you admit that the danger is out there and you are capable of falling prey to it, the next thing you need to do is get advice. Reliable, biblical, and ongoing advice.

"Without counsel, plans go awry, but in the multitude of counselors they are established" (Proverbs 15:22).

I like to refer to this as an accountability system. The best accountability partners you could ever have in life are your parents. I know some of you think your parents are the worst choice because they don't trust you or are very negative about the possibility of you dating, but there are several reasons why you need to make this accountability system work. The first and foremost reason: Your parents love you. They are going to look out for your best interests.

Having your parents as accountability partners will be a way for you to grow closer to them. As you discuss these issues with them, they can love you through your decisions and hold you accountable to being pure.

If you happen to have parents who don't care if you sleep around, you need to make an important decision on your own. Do you want God's best for yourself, or *your* best?

No matter what your parents allow you to do, you will still

pay the same consequences if you sin. Blaming your parents will not be a good enough excuse when you face God.

Remember, if you really want to be pure, which I assume you do since you are reading this book, it is going to take work and sacrifice. This includes working at relationships with those to whom you are going to be accountable. Yes, it is a lot of work, but keep in mind the lethal consequences of not doing what you should to stay pure.

Whomever your accountability partners are, they need to be people with whom you can be totally honest and who can be honest with you. You will need to share intimate information with them, and they must have the freedom to tell you their honest feelings about you, your friends, and the relationships you are in. Possibilities for an accountability partner include a youth pastor, a friend, a teacher, or a youth worker in the church.

There is nothing wrong with having more than one accountability partner. For example, your close friends are with you on a daily basis and know a lot about you. They can help you with certain decisions. But on the other hand, adults are authority figures with more life experience than your peers, and they are able to help you see things from a different perspective.

These accountability partners are crucial because they serve several purposes:

- PRAYER—They are people with whom you can pray. They can pray for wisdom, self-control, protection, and God's leading in everything you do and say. Most importantly, your accountability partner should be praying that God would bring godly friends into your life. You don't want to have anything to do with someone who will only bring you down.

- ASK TOUGH QUESTIONS—Your accountability partner needs to have the freedom to ask you the hard questions. He or she needs to ask you about your weaknesses, what is going wrong in a relationship, and whether you are experiencing any temptations or struggles. Are you struggling in your goal of staying pure? Have you sinned, gone too far? Is he or she pushing you to sin?

    This talk should occur on a very regular basis. This is why it is important to have an accountability partner who is already very much a part of your life—someone that you see regularly. Temptation is everywhere and always trying to work its way into your life, so the more often you can meet with your accountability partner, the better.

- SPIRITUAL GROWTH—Your accountability partner can keep a close watch on your relationship with God. Praying, reading, and studying the Bible together will help you develop the internal tools to remain pure. Spending regular time in spiritual development is vital to developing the strength and discipline necessary to live a sexually pure life. The benefits from such time together will assist you in your growth for years to come.

- INTERVIEW—When someone wishes to date you, your accountability partner can first collect a full set of fingerprints, a skin sample, and maybe a couple of teeth for identification if something happens. Only kidding! Your accountability partner's help is as simple as conducting an interview with anyone who expresses interest in dating you. Your partner can find out more about him or her, even asking about his or her intentions.

    Remember, having an accountability system will help you

be honest and aware of your weaknesses. Don't let temptation sneak up on you because you can't face up to your struggles.

"Search me, O God, and know my heart; Try me, and know my anxieties; And see if there is any wicked way in me, And lead me in the way everlasting" (Psalm 139:23–24).

We need to ask God to reveal our sins to us and give us strength and discipline to deal with them. We need to be totally aware of our weaknesses and shortcomings. I have listed a few questions for you to ask yourself that may help you identify your weaknesses.

- What sexually immoral behavior do you think about doing?
- What types of people are you most attracted to?
- Do you look at pornography in any form?
- Are there television shows that you watch simply because of the sexual content or how the people are dressed?
- Is there music that you listen to because of its sexual content?
- Is there a friend or friends at school that you find yourself lusting after?
- Are you being tempted in a relationship right now to do something you know is wrong or you feel uncomfortable doing because you feel it might lead to something else?
- Is there someone who is interested in getting sexually closer to you?

Think about these issues and talk to someone about them. Get advice on what you can do to prevent any of these situations from getting worse or happening at all.

To remain sexually pure, you have to come up with your own personal convictions, too. Just because you're reading this book doesn't mean you're ready to face the world. You have to take a personal stand on all the issues before you get in a situation that requires a decision. You need to know your own boundaries before such a situation arises, or else it's too late. Ask yourself:

- Do you have a strong conviction about how far you will go when it comes to sex?
- What are your beliefs about sex, kissing, and holding hands?
- When are you at the point of lusting and beginning to lust?
- When you go out with friends, are you always aware of the plan for the night? For example, are people coupling up?
- What are your friends' ideas on dating, love, sex, etc.?
- Are you aware of the spiritual maturity of the people you hang around with? Are they aware of what you believe?
- What do you believe about abortion and homosexuality?
- What does love mean?

Satan will always keep temptations in front of you. Once you begin hanging out with members of the opposite sex, there are certain warning signs you need to keep an eye out for. These warning signs will help you know if temptation is about to strike.

FANTASIZING

What do you find yourself thinking about when you are daydreaming? Are you thinking about someone so much it is distracting you from functioning? If you have a crush on someone, is it normal to think about him or her more than someone whom you don't have a crush on? If your thoughts have become so consuming that you cannot function, there is a problem. Once they begin to focus on doing sinful things, there is an even bigger problem.

Do you or your friends have a desire to be in secluded places?

Is there anyone trying to get you to go somewhere alone with him or her? Do you find yourself desiring to be alone with that person when you know that is unwise?

Proverbs 6:27 says, "Can a man take fire to his bosom, And his clothes not be burned?"

In other words, you cannot flirt with sin and not get hurt. It doesn't even have to be your fault or your idea to play with fire, because it will still burn everyone the same.

Touching by accident

Have you ever felt a hand brush across a part of your body and wondered, *How did that happen?* Sometimes it is an accident, and I will encourage giving someone the benefit of the doubt one time. But the second time, you can assume that it was intentional. This is a sign of more "accidents" and sexual pressure to come.

Preoccupied with clothing and appearance

How long does it take you to get dressed? How many times are you adjusting and readjusting your clothes so you show just enough to be noticed? There is nothing wrong with looking good, but you can go too far to attract attention. This turns into pornography when you are dressing and acting in a way to excite someone sexually.

Even if you take all of these precautions, you still might find yourself in a sticky situation. That is when you are going to need an emergency escape plan. The key is to escape when you think something is going to happen, rather than waiting around to find out if it does.

Before I outline a few ideas, let me say that this applies to guys just as much as girls. So much is always made of a girl's purity, yet guys have the same requirements for sexual purity that we place on girls. To make that point clear, I want us to look at the story of Joseph. See Genesis, chapter 39.

Joseph was working for Potiphar, a leader in Egypt. Potiphar had trusted all of his household matters to Joseph. Joseph was a desirable man. He was popular and handsome. Potiphar's wife had a thing for Joseph, too. She wanted to get close to Joe in a bad way, and the Bible says that she cast longing eyes on him. In other words, she began trying to seduce him with "that look."

Genesis 39:6–7 says, "And Joseph was handsome in form and appearance. Now it came to pass after these things that his master's wife cast longing eyes on Joseph, and she said, 'Lie with me.'"

What's a brother to do? In today's world, there's a lot of pressure on guys to sleep with their girlfriends, or they risk being labeled as gay. But there is only one person's opinion you should ultimately care about. Joseph had one person to please, and that was God alone.

"But he refused and said to his master's wife, 'Look, my master does not know what is with me in the house, and he has committed all that he has to my hand. There is no one greater in this house than I, nor has he kept back anything from me but you, because you are his wife. How then can I do this great wickedness, and sin against God?' And so it was, as she spoke to Joseph day by day, that he did not heed her, to lie with her or to be with her. But it happened about this time, when Joseph went into the house to do his work, and none of the men of the house was inside, that she caught him by his garment, saying, 'Lie with me.' But he left his garment in her hand, and fled and ran outside. And so it was, when she saw that he had left his garment in her hand and fled outside, that she called to the men of her house and spoke to them, saying, 'See, he has brought in to us a Hebrew to mock us. He came in to me to lie with me, and I cried out with a loud voice' " (Genesis 39:8–14).

When you feel you are in danger of being taken advantage of, you need to know what your escape strategy is. You must be prepared *ahead of time* for how you will get out of a bad situation.

Just because someone is pressing you or pushing up on you or sweatin' you or whatever you want to call it, it does not mean you have to give in. That excuse is never going to satisfy your parents, your friends, or God. Nowhere in the Bible does it say that sex before marriage is allowed if you are asked over and over again. God's Word is true and faithful, and if we obey we will be blessed. If we disobey we will pay consequences. Here are a few things to keep in mind.

1. DON'T WORRY ABOUT HURTING FEELINGS.

Never worry about hurting someone's feelings in a situation like this. When you say no, say it loud and clear and get out of there. Don't be intimidated into changing your mind.

Even though Potiphar's wife was offended when Joseph rejected her and she had him thrown in jail, Joseph still did the right thing and was rewarded later.

2. DEFEND YOURSELF.

Once you have an escape plan, you must next be prepared to defend yourself. Run, yell, scream, fight, punch, or do whatever is necessary to protect yourself. If you get out of the car, don't get back in. This is why it is important never to be alone with someone, no matter how much you trust him. If you are alone, it is going to be your word against his. In Joseph's case, he was falsely accused and convicted of something he did not do.

3. ALWAYS HAVE A BACKUP PLAN TO GET HOME.

Carry money for a phone call, cab, bus, whatever. If affordable, a cell phone is a good idea. Come to think of it, bringing another couple on the date in the first place is an even better idea.

When Joseph refused the advances of Potiphar's wife, she started pulling his clothes off! Joseph's quick feet were his escape plan. Always remember: When in doubt, run!

> *First Corinthians 6:18 says, "Flee sexual immorality. Every sin that a man does is outside the body, but he who commits sexual immorality sins against his own body."*

Satan is relentless in his attack; therefore, you must be just as relentless in your willingness to perfect your ability to escape. I have outlined some basic ideas and principles to help you develop your own system of resisting temptation and escaping sin. Remember, sex carries with it lifelong consequences. So do your best to perfect your ability to resist.

DISCUSSION QUESTIONS

1. List five people who could be your accountability partners.

_____

_____

_____

_____

_____

2. What reasons would prevent you from asking your parents to be your accountability partners?

_____

_____

3. What could you do to make it work better with your parents?

_____

_____

4. What would be the benefits of having your parents hold you accountable?

_____

_____

5. List five safe activities you can do as alternatives to exclusively dating one person.

_____

_____

_____

_____

_____

I DON'T WANT
YOUR SEX FOR NOW

CHAPTER 9

BUT I DO WANT

TO BE YOUR

FRIEND

When my daughter was three years old, someone gave her the black Ken and Barbie dolls. Barbie has the Diana Ross hair all the way down to her ankles. Ken is pretty smooth, too. He has a little six-pack stomach and a chiseled plastic body, a little Jherri Curl and a mustache. One day my daughter said to me, "Daddy, this is my man." I got a little upset because when you have a little girl, *you* are her man. You are her boyfriend and she is your girlfriend. As a matter of fact, when I took my daughter to a movie once, I said, "You are going on a date with me." You know, little father and daughter date, and she said, "You're already married." She took it literally.

I care for her, I love her, and when she gets married I will give her away and give that responsibility to another man. So when she told me that this Ken doll was her man, it hurt me. That night, when she went to bed, I went in to the toy box to have a conversation with the brother. I grabbed him and said, "So . . . you're dating my daughter. You got a job? Are you a Christian?" He did not respond. So I unscrewed his head, his arms, his legs—and she came in and there he was, just his torso. It was not a pretty sight.

My point of the story is this: Ken doesn't know anything about women. He is only a plastic doll. And when I thought of my daughter dating somebody, it bothered me because she was only three years old at the time. It wasn't time for me to start considering those kinds of things. But the day is going to come when she is going to pick a man. The day is going to come when both my daughters are going to decide to date.

What will I do when a real Ken comes knocking on our door? Even more importantly, what will you do when someone comes along? Are you ready for that person? Do you know what kind of person you are looking for? Do you know how you can attract the right person?

There is a process of getting to know people of the opposite sex, getting in touch with your likes and dislikes of people, and preparing yourself for Mr. or Mrs. Right. This chapter will get you started on that process.

I want to share some principles about having a relationship with someone of the opposite sex, and I am going to draw these principles from a story in the Bible, found in the book of Ruth.

The two main characters, Boaz and Ruth, are going to meet,

get engaged, and eventually get married. Let me refer to Boaz as Bo.

What's ironic is that there is no real dating process that they follow. There is no sexual immorality between them. One of them is not luring the other through dressing in a seductive manner. But some very interesting things happen despite the lack of planning on their part.

This chapter will teach the guy readers how to get a woman to bow at his feet. This is exactly what Ruth does to Bo. Yes, she gets on the ground and bows at his feet. But I must warn you, it is not what you think. As a matter of fact, it is going to require you fellas reading this book to make some serious changes in your way of thinking about women, because this kind of relationship will require having respect and humility for the females in your life.

Isn't having a woman bow at his feet something so many men would love to have happen? Chances are, there are not that many guys reading this book that are man enough to get a woman to bow at his feet God's way, at least today. But hopefully, after you finish this book and put into practice the things it teaches, you will have that experience.

On the other hand, Bo vows to do everything that Ruth ever asked him to do. Wow! What is the catch here? Again, I don't know many women who have what it takes to get a good man to say and follow through on that kind of promise, but much of what is required is in this book, as well. There are valuable lessons in this story for young people who are seeking love and relationships.

Since I know getting a woman to bow at a guy's feet is of interest to everyone, let me start there. Ladies, as you read this, take notes on how Bo treats Ruth and don't allow yourself to get involved with anyone that does not have this kind of a heart.

In the Bible, Boaz says to Ruth, " 'You will listen, my daughter, will you not? Do not go and glean in another field, nor go from here, but stay close by my young women [the women who worked for him]. Let your eyes be on the field which they reap, and go after them. Have I not commanded the young men not to touch you? And when you are thirsty, go to the vessels and drink from what the young men have drawn' " (Ruth 2:8–9).

Ruth was married at one time, but her husband died. She went to live with her mother-in-law, but they were very poor. As a result, she found herself gleaning grain in the field. Gleaning was a practice of walking behind the farmers to pick up whatever they accidentally dropped on the ground. By law, the farmers could not pick it back up and sell it. They had to leave it for the poor people.

Now, I want you to picture this. Ruth is on her hands and knees. She is "grubbin' " on the ground. She is putting food in her little bag and in her shawl. She is scared, she is dirty, she is desperate, and here comes Bo.

Guess what Bo does? Before I tell you what he does, let me tell you what he doesn't do. He doesn't come over and say "Yo, baby, what's your name? Me and you can make it." He doesn't rap to her. Instead, he finds out what her needs are. He then blesses her according to her needs.

Guys, do you know what the needs of women are? Clueless, huh? Well this is your lifelong quest: to find out what a woman wants in a relationship and become a master at providing it regularly and unselfishly.

We guys know what our own needs are, and we think that women have the same needs—but we are not even close. Oh no! To understand their needs takes a lifetime. I have been married sixteen years, and I still have a lot to learn.

It takes a lifetime of learning because we don't *want* to know what the needs of the opposite sex are. We're selfish and consumed with our own needs and wants. This is where Jesus comes in.

> *The Bible says in Philippians 2:3–4, "Let nothing be done through selfish ambition or conceit, but in lowliness of mind let each esteem others better than himself. Let each of you look out not only for his own interests, but also for the interests of others."*

This principle of looking out for the interests of others is no more important than when in a relationship between a man and woman. If you're smart, you won't wait to begin when you get married. This is something you must practice for years and make part of your very character.

Now, look again at Bo's words. He says, "I'm going to bless you. I know you're thirsty. Guess what? I took care of that. I know you're hungry. I took care of that. I know you're scared. I took care of that. Stay by my young women, and I told those men over there to leave you alone. When you want water, it's over there. If you want food, it is right there." Bo took care of everything. Fellas, are you that kind of guy?

Then Ruth "fell on her face, bowed down to the ground, and said to him, 'Why have I found favor in your eyes, that you should take notice of me. . . ?'" (Ruth 2:10).

Fellas, do you want a girl to bow to you? You'd better bow to her first. You'd better bless her first according to what God tells you to do. I'm not just talking about going out and buying girls gifts. I'm not saying that at all. What I'm saying is when you see a girl you like, you ask God, "What do you want me to do?" Most of the time He is going to tell you to walk the other way, that you're not ready. But if He does have you talk to her, you'd better remember that she is not there to serve you. She is not there to be your sex partner. You are there to love her and respect her. Remember, *loving her is helping her obey God.* There are no sexual perks and benefits. That comes when you put the ring on her finger.

If there were a guy with a reputation for blessing women according to God's Word, a guy who had a reputation for loving women according to God's Word, he would never have a problem getting a date. Why? Because all the women would know that he was safe. They would know that he would not take advantage of them. He wouldn't be slick. He wouldn't manipulate them. He would bless them. And that's what a woman wants.

The other important thing to note is that before Bo approached Ruth, he checked out her background. Ruth 2:11 says, "And Boaz answered and said to her, 'It has been fully reported to me, all that you have done for your mother-in-law since the death of your husband, and how you have left your father and your mother and the land of your birth, and have come to a people whom you did not know before.'"

Ya know what Bo is saying? "Ruth, I know all about you. Matter of fact, I did a background check on you, and everybody knows what you have done for your mother-in-law."

If you are going to hang out with someone, do a background check. Find out if they are a Christian. Find out if they are sold out to God. Find out how they treated the other people they dated. Save yourself a headache. Don't just go out with somebody because they ask you. Take your time.

THE BEST WAY TO GET A GOOD PERSON IS TO BE A GOOD PERSON.

Want to get a good guy? Be a good girl. Want to get a good girl? Be a good guy.

When I say good, I don't mean better than the neighborhood idiot or criminal. I mean someone who loves God. Someone who hungers and thirsts for the things of God. Someone whom God can call on to build His kingdom at any time. Someone who makes a commitment to being holy because God is holy.

How much growing up do you need to do? How close and solid is your relationship with the Lord, and what do you need to improve?

If you are plastic and fake, you will probably attract a plastic and fake person. If you are sincere, real, and love God, you will probably attract and not settle for anything but someone who is sincere, real, and in love with God. At least you will know what someone like that looks and acts like.

I used to lead a Bible study at my house. There were four girls that used to come together. Three of them came in their pumps, stylish hair, makeup, and spandex pants. But one of them came dressed modestly. It was like Larry, Moe, and Curly, and then the other girl named Diane.

Every week I would watch them, and they were always

together, but Diane was different from the other three. So I asked this kid on my street to tell me about Diane. He told me, "Oh, she's a good girl." I said, "That is all I want to know."

What do others says about you? What is your reputation? It could be that your perception of yourself is not the same as what others think about you. You will attract what you are, not necessarily what you want to be. Having a good reputation will help in attracting the right person, as well as in keeping the wrong person away.

REPEL THE WRONG PEOPLE.

When I was in high school, there were two girls I wanted to meet. They weren't necessarily the prettiest girls in the school, but there was something about them I found irresistibly attractive. All through high school I tried to get up the nerve to approach them, but whenever I got close, something inside me said, "Back off, chump." I couldn't figure it out! I never did meet them, but later I found out they were both Christians and virgins. I'm now convinced that it was their holiness and the power of God that kept me at a distance. I wasn't walking with the Lord then, and I had no good thoughts in me! Those girls were gifted with animal repellent.

Your relationship with God will have a big effect on the quality of person you choose for yourself and the quality of person who is interested in you.

Ladies, here is the part you have been waiting for. Bo says in Ruth 3:11, "And now, my daughter, do not fear. I will do for you all that you request, for all the people of my town know that you are a virtuous woman." I'll say it again, *"all the people of my town know . . ."* I'll say it one more time, *"all the people of my town know . . .*" They don't *think*. They don't have to *guess*. They *know* that Ruth was a virtuous, godly, and praying woman. Ladies, that is it. If you send off vibes that you are a virtuous woman, you will attract the right kind of man, just like Ruth did.

There was a young girl in my youth group named Laura. She was in the twelfth grade, and one day she came to me discouraged and emotionally down. I asked her what was wrong. She said, "I don't have a date to the prom."

Laura was a godly woman and still is. I put my arm around Laura and I said, "Look around this room." We were standing in the youth room at church. "None of these guys in here is good enough for you. They know better than to try to ask you out." I was trying to tell her God had everything under control. He did not want her with the wrong person. "You are too godly," I told her. "But God has someone, and He will bring him in the right time and place."

Today Laura is married to a Boaz, a man who loves God. At that time, I understood that she wanted to go to the prom. But you know what? A lot of guys would not even approach her because they knew nothing was going to happen as far as sex. It saved her a bunch of headaches. The devil was trying to confuse her by saying, "You need to have a boyfriend like everyone else." But God was protecting her.

Always remember that the quality of your relationship with God will have a big effect on the quality of person you choose for yourself and the quality of person who is interested in you. Spending regular time in spiritual development is vital to developing the strength and discipline necessary to live a sexually pure life. That is why it is so important to be in spiritual agreement with any person that you become close friends with.

The Bible says in Amos 3:3, "Can two walk together, unless they are agreed?"

The number one area of agreement must be spiritual. You and your dating partner, first of all, must be committed to Jesus Christ.

Second Corinthians 6:14 says, "Do not be unequally yoked together with unbelievers. For what fellowship has righteousness with lawlessness? And what communion has light with darkness?"

These verses are crystal clear. Do not get close to someone whose spiritual father is not Jesus. Light and darkness have nothing in common. You will never see the two hanging out together anywhere at any time. This verse is not intended to imply that a Christian is better than a non-Christian. In no way should you think that a nonbeliever is not worthy or good enough to speak to a Christian. But when it comes to those you want to develop a deep relationship with, God commands that you do so with a believer.

God's commands, whether you completely understand or agree with them, are to be obeyed. Christianity is not a democracy where you can vote on what you want to obey. It is not a faith where you can pick and choose the guidelines that rule your life. God has not and never will ask your opinion on His Word.

This principle is seen very clearly in the life of King Solomon. He was the wisest and richest man ever to live, but women and sexual immorality were his downfall. He thought that he could get away with bending God's rules, but he was very, very wrong. His love for women and idols caused him to lose his kingdom.

"But King Solomon loved many foreign women, as well as the daughter of Pharaoh: women of the Moabites, Ammonites, Edomites, Sidonians, and Hittites—from the nations of whom the Lord had said to the children of Israel, 'You shall not intermarry with them, nor they with you. For surely they will turn away your hearts after their gods.' Solomon clung to these in love. And he had seven hundred wives, princesses, and three hundred concubines; and his wives turned away his heart. For it was so, when Solomon was old, that his wives turned his heart after other gods; and his heart was not loyal to the Lord his God, as was the heart of his father David" (1 Kings 11:1–4).

It was the women Solomon chose to hang out with that turned his heart away from the Lord, just as God had warned him would happen.

God knows what He is talking about; therefore, make sure that the person who wants to be your special friend is more in love with Jesus than he or she is with you.

The following legend describes this valuable lesson well.

There was a young man who was shipped overseas for service in World War II. The three long years he was away from America were lonely, eased only by the letters he exchanged with a woman he had never met. They wrote to each other for three years. He never heard this woman's voice except in the letters; he never saw a photograph of her, and yet he fell in love with her. He fell in love with her spirit, and he fell in love with the person who was writing to him.

When the war ended and he returned home, he decided he had to meet her. He wrote, "I feel I'm in love with you. I know I haven't seen you, but our hearts have been knitted together over these last three years."

She wrote back, telling him she loved him, too. In her letter she arranged a way for them to meet. "Come down to the train station at five o'clock," she wrote. "I will be the one with the red rose in my hand."

The young man was very excited. He was nervous, too, since he'd never seen her before, but he was sure that this was the woman for him based on her heart.

When the day finally arrived, he got dressed up and went to the train station. Right away he saw a beautiful young woman in a green dress. He thought to himself, *I hope she's holding a red rose*. But he stopped, reminding himself that whether or not she was beautiful should not matter. He loved her for what was on the inside. Seeing that the woman in the green dress was not holding a rose, he kept walking.

Then he saw another woman. This woman was older and less attractive than the woman in the green dress. But in her hand was the red rose.

He approached her, took a swallow, then smiled, saying, "You are the woman with the red rose. I am so glad to meet you."

She returned the smile and answered, "Yes, I have the red rose, but I'm not the woman who wrote to you. The woman who wrote to you is over there in the green dress. She just wanted to check out your heart."

When the right man is with the right woman for the right reasons, it is a beautiful thing.

DISCUSSION QUESTIONS

1. If you want to get the right person, you must *be* the right person. List five changes in your spiritual life that need to occur in order to be the person you'd like to attract.

   _____

   _____

   _____

   _____

   _____

2. What can you do in order to bring about these changes?

   _____

   _____

3. If I were to do a background check on you by asking kids at your school about you, both friends and enemies, what would they say?

Strengths	**Weaknesses**
_____	_____
_____	_____
_____	_____

4. Boaz promised Ruth all that she asked because she was a virtuous woman. List five characteristics of a virtuous woman (see Proverbs 31), and then list five things you need to do in order to become more virtuous.

_____	_____
_____	_____
_____	_____
_____	_____
_____	_____

5. Because Boaz respected and honored Ruth, she bowed at his feet. She respected him back. List five ways to respect a woman God's way.

_____

_____

_____

_____

_____

6. What character traits do you need to work on to prevent attracting the wrong kinds of people?

_____

_____

_____

7. What aspects of your character will repel the people who don't have God's intentions in mind?

_____

_____

_____

CHAPTER 10

BUT DEFINITELY

LATER

You have been reading so much about why not to have sex. I have written about the dangers of lust and fulfilling your desires on your own. I have told you that sexual sin carries a lethal danger with it. But there must be some good news about sex—and there is. Sex—shameless oneness—is a beautiful thing. Of course it can only be truly shameless in the context of marriage. When two become one in the way God intended, it is more wonderful than anyone can imagine. But this shameless oneness is not only physical; it also entails spiritual implications. There are many word pictures found in the Bible that indicate the shameless oneness that a man and a woman experience is a metaphor for the spiritual shameless oneness we can have with

Christ through salvation. As you learn of this connection, I hope you will come to understand how every special shameless oneness is. My prayer is that you view sex the way God intended it to be viewed and give it the respect it deserves.

All through the Old Testament and the New Testament, the church and Israel are portrayed as the bride of Christ. In the Old Testament, God talks about how Israel would commit adultery against Him. God thinks of us—His followers—as a bride, and He is the groom.

The Bible says in Jeremiah 2:1–2, "The word of the Lord came to me, saying, 'Go and cry in the hearing of Jerusalem ... I remember you, the kindness of your youth, the love of your betrothal. ...' "

Ephesians 5:22–23 says, "Wives, submit to your own husbands, as to the Lord. For the husband is head of the wife, as also Christ is head of the church; and He is the Savior of the body."

Remember, a husband is to his wife as Christ is to the church, His followers.

Revelation 21:2 says, "Then I, John, saw the holy city, New Jerusalem, coming down out of heaven from God, prepared as a bride adorned for her husband."

Before you are a saint, you are an "ain't." An ain't is a saint without the "s" for being "saved." When you get saved, you enter into a covenant or agreement with God. It is a blood covenant. The blood is the blood of Jesus on the cross. Jesus died for your sin, and He shed His blood for you. You ask Him to forgive you, and His blood cleanses you of your sin. The Bible says it covers your sin. All through the Bible, from Genesis to Revelation, it says that "without the shedding of blood there is no forgiveness" (Hebrews 9:22 NIV).

Before Jesus died on the cross, God required a blood sacrifice for the forgiveness of sins. Blood from an animal had to be shed and offered. When Cain and Abel sacrificed to God, God accepted Abel's sacrifice but not Cain's. Why? Because Cain tried to give God wheat, the fruit of the ground. God rejected his offering because He required a blood sacrifice.

During the plagues against the Egyptians, God told the Jews to brush the blood of a lamb over their doorways so that the Angel of Death would pass over their homes. The blood sacrifice saved them. Today this celebration is called Passover.

For you to go into a covenant relationship with God as His bride, it is a "blood covenant." You are accepting Christ's redemption, believing that His blood that was shed for you will make you whole. As a Christian, you are made one with God.

When you consummate a marriage, you are sealing the oneness of the union of husband and wife, as well.

The Bible says in Genesis 2:24, "Therefore a man shall leave his father and mother and be joined to his wife, and they shall become one flesh."

If we look closer at what the Bible tells us about the creation of man and woman, we will see that there is more to this union than just sex.

Genesis 2:7, 21–23 says, "And the Lord God formed man of the dust of the ground, and breathed into his nostrils the breath of life; and man became a living being. . . . And the Lord God caused a deep sleep to fall on Adam, and he slept; and He took one of his ribs, and closed up the flesh in its place. Then the rib which the Lord God had taken from man He made into a woman, and He brought her to the man. And Adam said: 'This is now bone of my bones And flesh of my flesh; She shall be called Woman, Because she was taken out of Man.' "

God used Adam's rib to create a woman. God did not make the woman from the man's foot, possibly so he would not consider her something to be walked on or abused. He did not make the woman from the man's head, possibly to prevent the woman from thinking that she was above the man. The Bible tells us that God made the woman from Adam's rib.

Why do you think He did that? Let's take a look at some possible answers:

- *The rib is on the side of the man.* A man is supposed to walk side by side with his wife for life.
- *The rib is under the protective arm of the man.* Have you ever seen guys with their arms around their girlfriends and it looks like they have them in a choke hold? When you put your arm around your wife, you are representing to those looking on that you are there to care for, protect, support, and encourage.
- *The rib protects the man's heart.* I cannot tell you how many times my wife has protected my heart. She has the ability to know when someone is "sweet" on her man. She also has the ability to warn me about these types of women. There have been times after a service at church that a suspicious woman would approach me about how the service was "so moving," and my wife would be standing there thinking, *You need to move on out of here.* As soon as the other woman walked away,

my wife would look at me and say, "Stay away from her." She knows and sees things that I don't see. While getting out of my car at the airport one day, my son yelled out the window, "Dad, don't let any ladies get you." My wife has trained my kids to pray for me in this area. She protects my heart.

• *There is life in the rib.* In case you did not know, your blood is produced in the bones. When you were born, most of the bones in your body produced your blood. As you grew into an adult, most of the bones lost their ability to produce blood except the bones in your thighs, your sternum, and your rib cage.

God took a life-producing bone in order to make the woman, a life-giving human. Let me explain it this way. The woman, who was created by different materials than the man, was designed with a different purpose. Don't get me wrong, she wasn't created only to have babies, but I do consider this an awesome privilege. The Bible tells us in the Psalms that God forms us.

> *"For You have formed my inward parts; You covered me in my mother's womb. I will praise You, for I am fearfully and wonderfully made; Marvelous are Your works, and that my soul knows very well. My frame was not hidden from You, When I was made in secret. . . ." (Psalm 139:13–15).*

My friends, there is so much about sex and relationships that we might never know until we get to heaven, but trust that God has it all figured out. He has designed a way that two people can become one, and it so happens that this shameless oneness is in many ways a mirror image of the shameless oneness we have with Him. Jesus has taken away our shame and nailed it to the cross. Since He has taken away our shame and guilt, don't add shame back into your life by abusing this awesome gift of sex that He gave us. Make a decision to wait until the proper time to experience this shameless oneness with your spouse.

DISCUSSION QUESTIONS

1. How does this comparison of sex and salvation change your opinion about sex before marriage?

   _____

   _____

2. From what you have read in this book so far, how have your views on sex changed?

   _____

   _____

3. How do you think that waiting for shameless oneness with the one you marry will enhance the shameless oneness you have with Jesus?

   _____

   _____

4. What comparisons do you think there are between the relationship between two people who are married and the relationship between Jesus and a Christian?

   _____

   _____

CHAPTER 11

B U T   I   D O   W A N T

J E S U S '   L O V E

A N D

F O R G I V E N E S S

My girlfriend and I have been dating for three years, and we have been sexually active in the past. We have since decided not to have sex until we get married. When that happens, can my girlfriend wear a white dress?"

This was a question I got from a young man who had a legitimate concern about his future. Some of you may have similar concerns. Maybe you are not on the verge of getting married, but will God forgive you so that you can wear white at your wedding? (Wearing white represents purity.)

Even though I had been sexually active from my teen years until I gave my life to Christ, my wife wore a white dress and I wore a white suit at our wedding. My wife and I had lived together and sinned sexually, but once we gave our lives to Jesus, we stopped having sex until the night we were married. God restored our sexual purity.

Before you can move on in your life, especially if you have sinned sexually, you must be willing and able to properly receive and experience the cleansing forgiveness of God.

What is forgiveness? The Bible teaches that forgiveness is an act committed by God. It is an act of His cleansing, renewing, and changing from one thing to another. It is the act of excusing or pardoning another in spite of his sins, shortcomings, and errors. The Bible tells us that only God can forgive us of our sins.

Luke 5:21 says, "Who can forgive sins but God alone?"

People can forgive the things you have done to them, but only God can remove the eternal penalty of sin, which is death in hell. Forgiveness involves God forgetting the action and never remembering it or bringing it up again.

Hebrews 10:17 says, "Their sins and their lawless deeds I will remember no more."

God is not one to bring up the past once He has forgiven you. Satan will constantly bring up your past and make you feel as though nothing has changed in your life. People will remind you of your sin all the time. Your brothers, sisters, parents, and friends will bring up the past, but God will not. God not only forgets our sin, but He no longer holds us responsible to pay the penalty. He cleanses us from all unrighteousness related to our sin. In other words, He will cleanse your desire to sin again.

The Bible says in 1 John 1:9, "If we confess our sins, He is faithful and just to forgive us our sins and to cleanse us from all unrighteousness."

This is the most amazing thing about being forgiven: God gives us the power, ability, and desire to help us not sin anymore but instead to do things that are out of obedience to His Word.

The Bible says in Philippians 2:13, "For it is God who works in you both to will and to do for His good pleasure."

This forgiveness is clearly seen in a story recorded in the book of John. In the Bible, sexual sin was often punishable by a death sentence. In the following story, the woman was going to be stoned because she was caught in adultery, but Jesus had another plan in mind. As we study this story, ask God to reveal to you how much He wants to forgive and restore a pure heart in you. No matter what you have done, and I said *no matter what* you have done, God wants to forgive you. If He was willing to forgive the woman in this story, He cannot and will not deny you the same love.

In John chapter eight, the woman caught in adultery is facing death. Her accusers bring her to Jesus to see what He will do to her.

"But Jesus went to the Mount of Olives. But early in the morning He came again into the temple, and all the people came to Him; and He sat down and taught them. Then the scribes and Pharisees brought to Him a woman caught in adultery. And

when they had set her in the midst, they said to Him, 'Teacher, this woman was caught in adultery, in the very act. Now Moses, in the law, commanded us that such should be stoned. But what do You say?' " (John 8:1–5).

The woman in this story has no leverage. She was caught in the act, she is guilty, and she is as good as dead. Only you and God know what *you* have done, but let's say your life is a mess right now. You have sinned and sinned and have ignored all of God's warnings to stop. Here you are, standing before Him, guilty, wondering what is going to happen. Well, what He does is going to depend on what you do.

First, we know that we need to come to God ourselves instead of being brought to God by those who accuse and judge us. Your reading this book is evidence of you doing just that. At the end of this chapter, you will be given a chance to get things right with God and have all of your sins erased. Prepare to humble yourself before God and confess and repent of your sin. His mercy is immeasurable, and it is there for you in your time of need.

Hebrews 4:15–16 says, "For we do not have a High Priest who cannot sympathize with our weaknesses, but was in all points tempted as we are, yet without sin. Let us therefore come boldly to the throne of grace, that we may obtain mercy and find grace to help in time of need."

First, you must accept that you have sin in your life.

First John 1:8 says, "If we say that we have no sin, we deceive ourselves, and the truth is not in us."

Second, you must realize that your sin, like everyone else's, has a penalty attached to it.

Romans 6:23 says, "For the wages of sin is death, but the gift of God is eternal life in Christ Jesus our Lord."

First John 1:9 says, "If we confess our sins, He is faithful and just to forgive us our sins and to cleanse us from all unrighteousness."

Now, do you want to know what Jesus decided to do with the woman caught in adultery? After Jesus looked at the crowd and wrote in the dirt, He stood up and said, " 'He who is without sin among you, let him throw a stone at her first' " (John 8:7).

It is God who judges. He judges according to His Word, not man's opinion. God is not influenced by the opinion of someone else about your sin. He loves you and wants to forgive and cleanse you. He knows everything there is to know about your life. Therefore, don't worry about what people say. Worry about what God says and what He's required from you. God's requirements are clear and don't change. His Word is not old-fashioned, because God lives outside of time. He does not change with the cultures or traditions of man. His laws are never irrelevant because of what you hear and see on television, music videos, or the movies. His laws are based on eternal principles.

The Bible says in Matthew 24:35, "Heaven and earth will pass away, but My words will by no means pass away."

Fear God and obey His commandments only. After Jesus told the crowd to go ahead and throw stones if they were without sin, all of the woman's accusers walked away. They knew that they had no right to condemn this woman. No one was without sin.

> *"When Jesus had raised Himself up and saw no one but the woman, He said to her, 'Woman, where are those accusers of yours? Has no one condemned you?' She said, 'No one, Lord.' And Jesus said to her, 'Neither do I condemn you; go and sin no more'"* *(John 8:10–11).*

If you read the words of Jesus carefully, you will notice a few important things. Jesus gave her a new name. He called her "woman."

Can you imagine the names this woman was called because of her sin? Harlot, adulteress, dead girl walking. But Jesus called her woman. When you walk with Jesus, your name, your title, your identity changes.

> *The Bible says in 2 Corinthians 5:17, "Therefore, if anyone is in Christ, he is a new creation; old things have passed away; behold, all things have become new."*

In other words, once you decide to receive forgiveness from Christ and walk with Him, your life changes. Things become new again. The Bible says that we are saints, a royal priesthood, chosen people, His workmanship, and His children. These new names result from a new relationship with God. This new relationship with God brings with it a new purpose in life, a new standard for living.

SIN NO MORE

When we receive God's forgiveness, He gives us a new direction in life. This change in direction for life means that you must be willing to forgive others just as you have been forgiven. This change in life's direction is called repentance. True forgiveness does not happen without true repentance. God is not a sucker. He knows the heart of man. This forgiveness I have been talking about is much more than just being forgiven for sinning sexually. It is being forgiven for all of your sin. The type of forgiveness I am talking about is complete and eternal. It is the forgiveness of salvation.

During the years of 1993–96, youth ministries nationwide were holding True Love Waits rallies for their youth. The goal was to encourage young people to make a covenant with God to remain sexually pure until they were married. I was asked to speak at about ten such rallies across the country and enjoyed speaking at them. But whenever I was asked to speak, I accepted on the one condition that I be allowed to share the Gospel. In most cases, I met no opposition. But every now and then, someone would challenge my request and ask why I was so convinced I needed to do an altar call. The first reason was that I am an evangelist at heart and want to see everyone get saved. But there was another reason. What good does it do to not have sex and still go to hell? Just because you are not having sex does not mean that God is going to forgive your sins and allow you into heaven.

The Bible says in John 3:3, "Jesus answered and said to him, 'Most assuredly, I say to you, unless one is born again, he cannot see the kingdom of God.'"

Nowhere does it say that if you abstain from sexual activity you will enter the kingdom of God. Yes, being sexually pure is a very vital part of being saved, but someone can withhold themselves from sex all of their life and still go to hell.

Another reason salvation is important is because upon

receiving Christ as your Savior, you receive the power to do the things God has required.

Yes, people have been able to resist temptation on their own, but there is no comparison to the power you receive when Jesus becomes your Lord and the Holy Spirit comes into your heart. Therefore, it is important for you to know that salvation is key to this process.

When you receive Christ into your heart, several things will happen in your life. God separates our sin from us as far as the east is from the west.

Psalm 103:11–12 says, "For as the heavens are high above the earth, so great is His mercy toward those who fear Him; As far as the east is from the west, So far has He removed our transgressions from us."

God knows we are hopeless and helpless without Him. He knows that we need Him and that without Him sin is going to happen and consume our lives. But He loves us and wants to cleanse us of our ugly past and prevent it from happening again. The passage continues and says,

"As a father pities his children, so the Lord pities those who fear Him. For He knows our frame; He remembers that we are dust" (Psalm 103:13–14).

Remember, part of being forgiven means walking and living as though you are forgiven. Being made to feel guilty after you have been forgiven is not from God but the devil.

The Bible says that you shall know the truth and the truth shall set you free. Reading the Bible, depending on the Bible, and meditating on the Bible are the best defenses against the lies of the devil.

Another important part of being forgiven is being able to forgive others. I have been asked by several people who are virgins if they should discount dating and marrying someone who has been with someone else sexually. Perhaps you have this same question. First, you must be willing to forgive that person just as God has forgiven him or her. In forgiving, you must be willing to forget this person's past and move on accepting him or her as a new person in Christ.

> The Bible says in Matthew 6:14–15, "For if you forgive men their trespasses, your heavenly Father will also forgive you. But if you do not forgive men their trespasses, neither will your Father forgive your trespasses."

If you want God to completely forgive you and give you a fair chance at a new start, you must be willing to forgive and love others in the same way. The Bible also challenges us not to judge someone lest we be judged.

> Matthew 7:1–5 says, "Judge not, that you be not judged. For with what judgment you judge, you will be judged; and with the same measure you use, it will be measured back to you. And why do you look at the speck in your brother's eye, but do not consider the plank in your own eye? Or how can you say to your brother, 'Let me remove the speck out of your eye'; and look, a plank is in your own eye? Hypocrite! First remove the plank from your own eye, and then you will see clearly to remove the speck out of your brother's eye."

In other words, don't determine that someone is less than

what they are based on your opinion of them. In this case, you could be judging the integrity, value, or worth of someone based on a mistake they made in the past. Instead, through the grace of God, you need to see them for what they could be in the Lord.

As you move forward in your life, take a moment right now and receive God's eternal and complete forgiveness. Pray this prayer and put an end to your guilt and shame. Allow God to give you your spiritual virginity back.

Dear God, I believe that I have sinned. The Bible says in 1 John 1:8, "If we say that we have no sin, we deceive ourselves, and the truth is not in us," and Romans 3:23 says, "For all have sinned and fall short of the glory of God." I believe that my sin will kill me, my dreams, and my hope unless I have Jesus in my life. The Bible says in Romans 6:23, "For the wages of sin is death, but the gift of God is eternal life in Christ Jesus our Lord."

But I believe that Jesus loves me. I believe that He is the Lord, died and risen from the dead for my sin. Jesus, please forgive all my sin and cleanse me from my unrighteousness.

Please give me a pure heart, one that fears and obeys your Word. Please restore my spiritual virginity to me. I commit my entire life as well as my sexual life to you and vow to save myself until marriage.

Thank you, Jesus.

DISCUSSION QUESTIONS

1. Are you worried about not being forgiven of past sexual sin?

_____

_____

_____

_____

2. Are you having a hard time forgiving others for what they have done in the past?

_____

_____

3. Is there some secret sin you have that you don't think Jesus will forgive?

_____

_____

4. Is there some secret sin that you need to talk to someone about in order to completely be set free from it? If so, talk to you parents, counselors, or someone you trust today.

_____

_____

CITATIONS

1. Press release: *The Center for Media and Public Affairs.*
2. Ibid.
3. Press release: *Screen Actors Guild Report,* "Casting the American Scene," December 1998.
4. Press release: *Parents Television Council,* "What a Difference a Decade Makes," March 30, 2000.
5. *www.gradingthemovies.com.*
6. Joellen Perry, *U.S. News and World Reports,* "Sex Sells, Sometimes," April 23, 2000.
7. *www.cnet.com,* "Sex on the Web," April 28, 1999.
8. Steven Watters, M.A., *www.family.com, Forrester Research,* "An Overview of Online Pornography."
9. *Wired News,* June 10, 1998.

Teen Devotionals From BHP

* *Discovery Workbook and Leader's Guide also available*

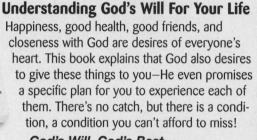